popstars

THE MAKING OF

hear'say

The OFFICIAL inside story by
MARIA MALONE

GRANADA

Author Acknowledgements

I am deeply grateful to all those who contributed to this book. First and foremost to Nigel Lythgoe, who unfailingly managed to return my calls and emails (and make space in the diary) when there were millions of other things to do. I am also grateful to Paul Adam (mind your language) and the brilliant Nicki Chapman. Thanks also to the *Popstars* production team – especially Maria Barlow, Louise Cowmeadow, Luke Dolan, Danny Fildes, Conrad Green, Claire O'Donohoe, David O'Neill and Andy Kelk. Also, to the hugely talented 33 who made it as far as Brixton.

Above all, my love and respect go to Noel, Myleene, Kym, Danny and Suzanne.
The world is yours – strength in unity!

Finally, eternal gratitude to all those who held my hand throughout, and made the top diving board a less lonely place.

'Popstars' is an LWT Production based on a Screentime Pty Ltd format

Executive Producer:	Nigel Lythgoe
Series Producer:	Conrad Green
Head of Production:	Jane Honeycombe
Producer/Directors:	James Breen, Danny Fildes, David O'Neill, Tim Quicke
Associate Producer:	Claire O'Donohoe
Judges:	Nigel Lythgoe, Nicki Chapman, Paul Adam
Voice Coach:	Annie Skates
Psychologist:	Conrad Potts

Granada Media would also like to thank the following for their help with this book: photographers Ken McKay and Jack Barnes; Ian Johnson, Shane Chapman and Penny McGuire from the LWT Press Office; Chris Herbert and Grant Logan of Safe Management, Alex Bertie of Polydor; and Nicky Paris, Russell Porter and Alastair Gourlay of André Deutsch.

Contents

Introduction Wanted: Popstars   4

The 33   8

The Brixton Workshop   12

Then there were five   44

Popstars at Home   48

Who's Who – The Band   52

The Band on The Band   62

Popstars at Work   64

Acknowledgements   78

Wanted: *Popstars*

10 August 2000. The ad in *The Stage* dwarfs the others on the page. In big, bold letters it reads, *Wanted: Popstars*. Have you got what it takes to be a star?

The Stage, the entertainment industry's weekly newspaper, often carries ads for new bands. What made this one different was that it was not just a trawl for talent. It was a *televised* trawl. The search for *Popstars* was not simply about finding a band. It was also about making a high-profile documentary series for ITV.

Word soon spread. Local newspapers ran the story. Regional television and radio shows announced where and when open auditions were being held. Thousands came forward. Just five would make it.

At the helm of the series was Nigel Lythgoe, Controller of Entertainment and Comedy for London Weekend Television and United. Even before the first audition Lythgoe – the man behind shows like *Gladiators*, *Barrymore* and *An Audience With* – knew he had the makings of a smash hit on his hands.

> **'They have to be able to stand up and sing... That may sound harsh, but that's the nature of the business.'**
> **NIGEL LYTHGOE**

Popstars had already proved a winning formula in Australia. When the series aired there, it launched the girl band Bardot, whose first single charted at Number One. *Popstars* was soon the most watched show in Oz.

Here, as the first auditions began, the *Popstars* phenomenon rapidly grew.

Over a period of six weeks thousands of hopefuls lined up at venues throughout the UK. Some arrived the night before and slept in the open just to be at the front of the queue.

The task of sifting good from bad fell to Nigel Lythgoe and fellow judges Paul Adam – director of A & R at Polydor records – and Nicki Chapman, Billie Piper's manager, and former publicist for the Spice Girls.

All three knew from the outset that the audition process would be tough. None anticipated just how tough. In among the (relatively few) brilliant and talented individuals who auditioned were those who could not sing to save their lives. Some were truly awful. Others simply lost their nerve when the moment came to perform.

'They *have* to be able to stand up and sing,' Lythgoe said later. 'That may sound harsh, but that's the nature of the business.'

At times, the judges' frustration was evident. In Belfast, where the turnout for the auditions was disappointingly low, Nigel Lythgoe was blunt. 'Your performances were poor. I don't think any of you were good enough,' he said.

In Birmingham, after a flurry of poor performers, he muttered, 'If they think they can sing they're either deaf or stupid.'

From the beginning, he was the straight-talking member of the panel. Yet what became apparent as the auditions wore on was that Lythgoe, more than anyone, was deeply moved by the efforts of the kids lining up to sing for him.

Popstars is about hopes and dreams. At times, watching those dreams shatter at close range, proved almost unbearable.

So you want to be a Popstar?

There is, it seems, no formula for becoming a pop star. It is all to do with a magical, indefinable ingredient called stardust.

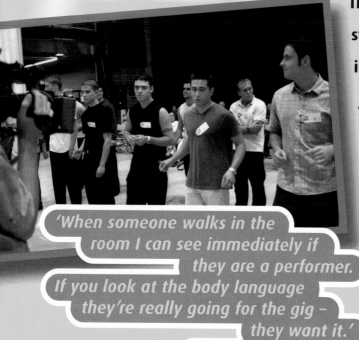

'It's a little bit of magnetism that draws you in. A look, a smile. Something that makes you want to be with them,' Lythgoe says.

Nicki Chapman agrees. 'When someone walks in the room I can see immediately if they are a performer. If you look at the body language they're really going for the gig – they want it.'

> '*When someone walks in the room I can see immediately if they are a performer. If you look at the body language they're really going for the gig – they want it.*'
> **NICKI CHAPMAN**

For Paul Adam, who looks after artists like Ronan Keating and S Club 7 for Polydor, the number one priority is a great voice. Of the three judges, he perhaps was most nervous about appearing on television. 'Mainly because I swear a lot when I speak,' he says.

Among the thousands who turned up at the early auditions were Noel Sullivan, Kimberley (Kym) Marsh, Danny Foster, Myleene Klass and Suzanne Shaw.

Only Suzanne was unreservedly enthusiastic about *Popstars* from the outset. The others were wary of a band manufactured specifically for television.

Noel, 20, was waiting on tables in a Latin American café in Cardiff when he heard about *Popstars*. Having recently returned home after a stint in cabaret in Ibiza, he was saving hard to move to London.

'I was going to audition for anything going,' he says. A friend spotted a story about *Popstars* in the *South Wales Echo* and tipped him off.

'It was like, "Do you want to be in the next S Club 7 or Steps?" ' he says, laughing. 'Er, no ..! I had quite strict ideas about music and I didn't want to be in a tacky pop band. I didn't see myself as the next H.'

Noel auditioned in Cardiff and was called back. He was one of 163 short-listed for two days of intensive auditions in Birmingham a few weeks later.

Danny, 21, from London, also had doubts about *Popstars* to begin with. 'I rang this number and it was like, "Hi – welcome to *Popstars*!" ' Danny hung up. He was tempted not to bother. 'I had flu and I really wasn't going to go,' he says.

At the time he was working as a part-time cleaner in an office block in Hackney, north London and singing in local pubs. 'I'd decided to take a year out and really give the singing a go,' he says. 'I didn't want to live with the regret that I hadn't tried.'

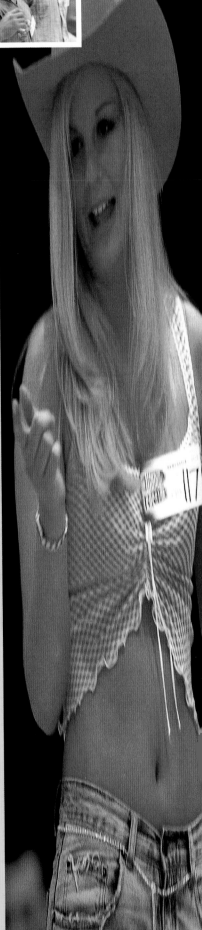

In Wigan, Kimberley, 24, was also reluctant to audition for *Popstars*. She knew nothing about it until her Dad saw a report on the local news. 'My Dad was really excited but I knew there were going to be thousands there and the chances were I wasn't going to get anywhere,' she says. Kym also knew that she was right on the edge of the upper age limit. She decided to give the auditions a miss. Luckily, her Dad was not about to take *no* for an answer.

The next day at 5.30a.m. Kym and her Mum were on their way to Manchester.

'I really wasn't expecting anything,' she says. 'I couldn't believe it when I got through to the call-backs. It was all thanks to my Mum and Dad.'

In nearby Bury in Lancashire, 19-year-old Suzanne had spotted the ad in *The Stage*.

She was already singing with an Abba tribute band called The Right Stuff, performing on the cabaret circuit. After 18 months she was looking for a change. She and Kym ended up at the same audition in Manchester.

Suzanne had done plenty of auditions in her time. She always did well, but not quite well enough. 'I would get down to the last five or the last two but I'd never get it,' she says. 'I'd end up thinking, why not me?'

Myleene, 22, from Norfolk, auditioned at the LWT studios in London. She was busy carving a successful music career for herself and had toured as a backing vocalist with Cliff Richard and

Michael Crawford (among others). She had performed in the stage show *Miss Saigon* and appeared on BBC's *Parkinson* show as a backing vocalist for KD Lang. A second appearance on *Parkinson* was in the offing – this time backing Robbie Williams. When *Popstars* came along Myleene was recording a TV show at LWT with Lily Savage. She says, 'I almost missed the auditions, but someone suggested I go along.' She laughs. 'Just as well – I ended up with my dream job!'

It was early October before the judges had their first short-list, comprising 163 names from the first round of auditions. In the course of two days at Birmingham's National Indoor Arena the number would drop by 130. The following week 33 hopefuls would gather in London for a five-day workshop, at the end of which just ten would remain.

As Myleene, Noel, Kym, Danny and Suzanne prepared to pack for the London workshop they couldn't know that their lives were about to change for good. Yet just a few weeks later they would be in a band – *the* band – starring in a hit TV series, and sharing a house together.

First, though, came the toughest audition of their lives.

The ⭐ 33

Finally, it's down to the last **33**, and time for the real **hard work** to start. Over **five** days, these 33 finalists will be put through their paces and at the end **the band** will emerge.

But **who** are the **33?**

'This is something I've wanted to do all my life.'

16

'I've got talent, I know that.'

1

'People are always telling me to get a proper job but I just love singing

6

13

'I ain't got a clue why I put myself through all this.'

11

'I wouldn't want to get into the band for something I'm not. This is me and you either like me or not.'

HAYLEY EVETTS.

'Thrown together with four other people? I'd love it!'

10

FRANK DOROLLO.

'My worst habit is making a joke out of everything.'

4

3

'I see this as my last chance for a career in pop.'

DAVID WILSON

8

'I would love to be able to say, "Look – here's me in a cheesey pop band!"'

7

NOEL SULLIVAN

JAMES MASON

'I see the band as a stepping stone to something else.'

15

5

'I've never felt confident that I would be picked.'

2

'I believe in God and I really believe God has got me here today.'

Gary Lewis

9

'I don't know how to do anything else.'

'Fame is what I want. I want to be successful. I want to do this.'

12

S. Colcon

CHARLOTTE GASKELL

'I didn't have any training, didn't go to drama school. No singing lessons, nothing.'

8

DANNY FOSTER,

14

'The pressure is on to be your best — you can't have a bad day in showbiz.'

M. C Heat

popstars

1 **DARIUS DANESH 20, FROM GLASGOW**
Tall, dark, handsome. Student/entrepreneur. Has a steady girlfriend, but making it into the band comes first.

2 **GARY LEWIS 21, FROM DARLASTON IN THE WEST MIDLANDS**
Funny, droll, determined. Deeply religious.

3 **DAVID WILSON 25, FROM GATESHEAD**
The oldest in the group. Warm, engaging, generous. Robbie lookalike.

4 **JAMES MASON 21, FROM KENT**
Sang a rude version of Britney's Baby One More Time at his first audition – by accident.

5 **KEVIN SIMM 20, FROM BLACKBURN**
Sings in a boy band. Once appeared on *Stars In Their Eyes* (as Simon Fowler singing The Riverboat Song). Single-minded, ambitious, serious.

6 **KIMBERLEY MARSH 24, FROM WIGAN**
Beautiful, bright, comical. A livewire. Singing and dancing since she was ten years old.

7 **NOEL SULLIVAN 20, FROM CARDIFF**
Witty, sharp, wicked impersonator. Big-hearted. Family comes first.

8 **DANNY FOSTER 21, FROM LONDON**
Easy going, laid-back. Huge voice. Discovered he could sing in a karaoke bar in Tenerife three years ago.

9 **SUZANNE SHAW 19, FROM BURY**
Blue-eyed blonde. Bubbly. Cute.

10 **FRANK DI ROLLO 23, FROM EDINBURGH**
Psychology student. Piercing green eyes.

11 **HAYLEY EVETTS 24, FROM BIRMINGHAM**
Easy going, slightly scatty. Works in a fancy-dress shop with her Mum.

12 **CHARLOTTE GASKELL 19, FROM LONDON**
Huge expressive eyes. Pierced belly button. Self-confessed chocoholic.

13 **KELLI YOUNG 18, FROM LONDON**
Strong, independent. Reckons *Popstars* auditions are the most gruelling she has ever done.

14 **MICHELLE HEATON 21, FROM NEWCASTLE**
Talkative, sensitive, smart, cheeky. Got down to the last 12 for the band Girl Thing.

15 **AKIYA, HENRY 21, FROM LONDON**
Actress, dancer, singer. Loud, wild, practical joker.

16 **IAN HARVEY 22, FROM SOUTHAMPTON**
Cheeky, chirpy chappie.

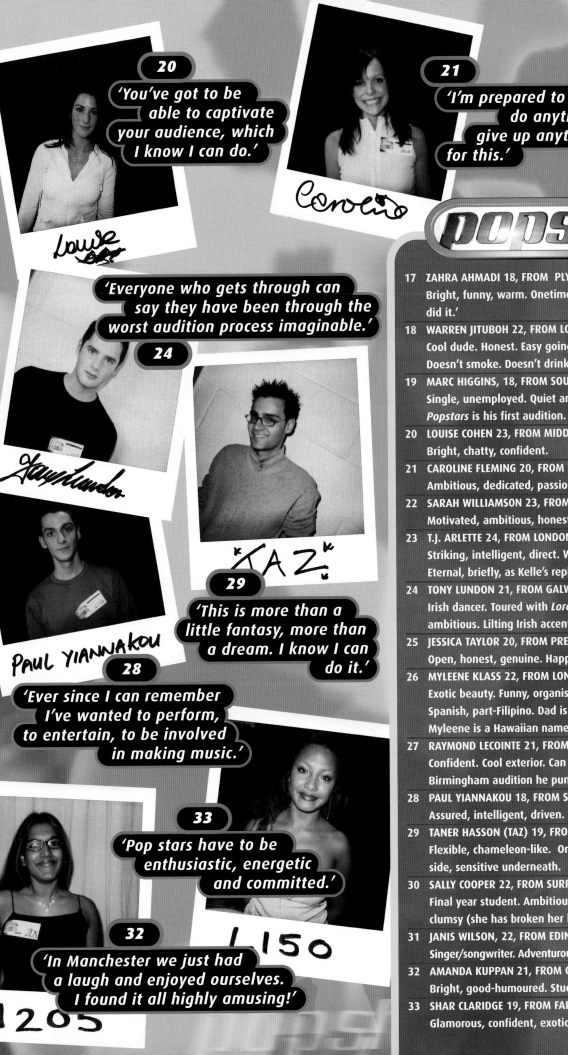

20 'You've got to be able to captivate your audience, which I know I can do.'

Louise

21 'I'm prepared to do anything and give up anything for this.'

Caroline

popstars

'Everyone who gets through can say they have been through the worst audition process imaginable.'

24

Tony Lundon

29 'This is more than a little fantasy, more than a dream. I know I can do it.'

TAZ

PAUL YIANNAKOU

28 'Ever since I can remember I've wanted to perform, to entertain, to be involved in making music.'

33

32 'Pop stars have to be enthusiastic, energetic and committed.'

'In Manchester we just had a laugh and enjoyed ourselves. I found it all highly amusing!'

L150

1205

17 ZAHRA AHMADI 18, FROM PLYMOUTH
Bright, funny, warm. Onetime diet fiend, 'you name it, I did it.'

18 WARREN JITUBOH 22, FROM LONDON
Cool dude. Honest. Easy going. Born-again Christian. Doesn't smoke. Doesn't drink.

19 MARC HIGGINS, 18, FROM SOUTHAMPTON
Single, unemployed. Quiet and reserved. Elvis lookalike. *Popstars* is his first audition.

20 LOUISE COHEN 23, FROM MIDDLESEX
Bright, chatty, confident.

21 CAROLINE FLEMING 20, FROM WIDNES
Ambitious, dedicated, passionate about singing.

22 SARAH WILLIAMSON 23, FROM LIVERPOOL
Motivated, ambitious, honest. Training to be a teacher.

23 T.J. ARLETTE 24, FROM LONDON
Striking, intelligent, direct. Witty and self-possessed. Joined Eternal, briefly, as Kelle's replacement (quit five days later).

24 TONY LUNDON 21, FROM GALWAY
Irish dancer. Toured with *Lord Of The Dance*. Good-looking, ambitious. Lilting Irish accent.

25 JESSICA TAYLOR 20, FROM PRESTON
Open, honest, genuine. Happy and secure.

26 MYLEENE KLASS 22, FROM LONDON
Exotic beauty. Funny, organised, intelligent. Mum is part-Spanish, part-Filipino. Dad is part-English, part-Austrian. Myleene is a Hawaiian name.

27 RAYMOND LECOINTE 21, FROM LONDON
Confident. Cool exterior. Can lose it under pressure (at the Birmingham audition he punched a toilet door!).

28 PAUL YIANNAKOU 18, FROM SURREY
Assured, intelligent, driven.

29 TANER HASSON (TAZ) 19, FROM ESSEX
Flexible, chameleon-like. One-off. Confident on the outside, sensitive underneath.

30 SALLY COOPER 22, FROM SURREY
Final year student. Ambitious, obsessively tidy. Alarmingly clumsy (she has broken her leg five times).

31 JANIS WILSON, 22, FROM EDINBURGH
Singer/songwriter. Adventurous, outgoing. (Quietly) confident.

32 AMANDA KUPPAN 21, FROM GLOSSOP IN DERBYSHIRE
Bright, good-humoured. Student.

33 SHAR CLARIDGE 19, FROM FAREHAM IN HAMPSHIRE
Glamorous, confident, exotic.

The Brixton Workshop

Be afraid... Be very afraid.

Day 1

Monday 10 October. A cold, grey morning. Commuters hurry along Brixton Road in south London barely aware of the coach easing its way through the rush-hour traffic. There are 33 passengers on board – 15 boys and 18 girls – all of whom have made it through the first stages of the *Popstars* auditions. The serious business of choosing the band is about to get underway.

Five tough days lie ahead – for the lucky ones, at least. Not everyone will make it beyond day one. Part of this final auditioning process involves a one-to-one session with the judges at the end of each day to find out who stays and who goes. By the end of the week just ten individuals will remain. Each day they will walk the Green Mile, a reference to the Tom Hanks film of the same name about prisoners on death row.

In the LWT rehearsal rooms everyone clusters round Nigel Lythgoe. The previous night he was up singing a karaoke version of I Will Survive at a party designed to break the ice. Now, as he spells out what lies ahead, there is little evidence of the party animal of just a few hours ago.

'This is going to be crunch week. This is where we have to decide,' he tells 33 anxious faces.

'At the end of the week we are going to give ten of you contracts, which you can have checked out by lawyers...' A mobile phone interrupts him. 'Will you turn that phone off *please*?' He grins... 'It's mine.' Laughter briefly breaks the tension. Everyone makes a mental note to switch off their own mobiles at the first opportunity.

The first day will concentrate on movement and harmonies. As Nigel runs through the schedule, choreographer Di Cook, vocal coach Annie Skates, and musical director Trevor Brown, look on.

Already the Green Mile has become the single most discussed topic. Someone has been spreading the word – falsely, it turns out – that there will be no Green Mile on the first day. Nigel is keen to put the record straight. 'It will happen *every* day,' he insists.

There is one more piece of news – over the course of the next few days they will be interviewed, one by one, for the *Popstars* book. As with everything else, the process will be on camera. 'If there's anything you don't want in the TV show come and tell me and we'll take it out,' he says. 'Then when you've gone we'll put it back in ...' Nervous laughter echoes round the room.

> 'If there's anything you don't want in the TV series come and tell us and we'll take it out. Then when you've gone we'll put it back in ...'
> **NIGEL LYTHGOE**

By 9.30a.m. the 33 are preparing to warm up under the watchful eyes of the judges. This is the final selection process. In less than seven hours the first wave of rejections will take place.

'I'm sorry some of you appear to be not at your best, with sore throats and so on,' says Nigel. 'But this business does not allow you to be ill. It *is* tough. You have to get up there and smile even when you're feeling sick. If you *are* ill, do your best.'

At the back of the group Sally Cooper, 22, allows herself a wry smile. Sally, a student and ex-model, is nursing cracked ribs and has turned up for the audition wearing impractical footwear. Her blue satin mules with spiky heels are far from ideal for a punishing warm-up. Nonetheless, she puts on a brave face.

'It really hurts if I laugh or sneeze or brush my teeth, but it's okay just now. The bruising's gone down. If it hurts I just stop,' she says.

Sally is used to coping with injury. After her first audition in Cardiff in August, her neck seized up. Before the second round of auditions in Birmingham, she fell down the stairs. She has broken her leg five times. She is, she admits, a walking disaster area. Even so, nothing – not even cracked ribs – will stop her from giving the audition 100 per cent.

'I'm dying for the big break,' she says without irony.

Equally determined is Janis Wilson, who went to the Glasgow audition after hearing about it on her local radio station. *Popstars* was her first audition. 'I'm really pleased to have got this far,' she says, a silver stud glinting on her tongue. 'I'm just enjoying it. It's a privilege to be in London. If I don't get it I can't dwell on it.'

By mid morning on Day One some dominant characters among the 33 are beginning to emerge, among them Darius Danesh, who auditioned in Glasgow. In the space of a few hours he has become everyone's big brother. Tall, good-looking, charismatic and charming, Darius – just 20, but with the self-possession of someone twice his age – is fast proving himself a born leader.

He is not at his best, however. Earlier he was sick. Now, sipping weak tea and looking pale, he admits he may have overdone things the week before. A student of English Literature and Philosophy at Edinburgh University, he also runs a thriving entertainment business. Juggling his many commitments can be a strain.

'I don't always fit everything in and I ran myself down last week,' he admits.

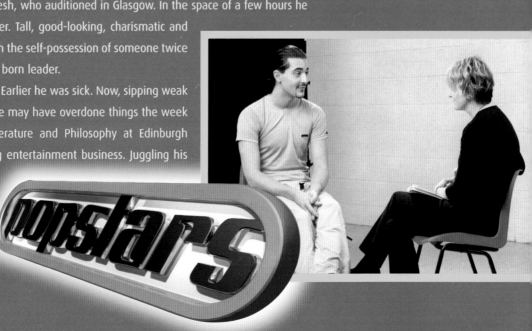

Darius

'I've always dreamed of performing with a group of people.'

At first sight, Darius is a hot favourite for the band. He appears to have all the right qualities. He has been singing and acting from an early age (appearing on stage in *Peter Pan* at the age of three). He is funny, engaging, bright and talented. But, is he enough of a team player? Is he just *too* tall? All three judges have reservations. Darius himself has no such doubts.

'I've always dreamed of performing with a group of people,' he says. 'There's an incredible amount of energy from a band, as opposed to just one person up there.'

At his Glasgow audition Darius, like James Mason, caught the judges' attention with a rude rendition of Britney's Baby One More Time – a song from the girls' list – prompting Nigel Lythgoe to describe him as, 'a bit of a cocky bugger.' There is a sense you could hurl any calamity in his path and he would calmly step over it. He is almost *too* articulate for a 20-year-old. It is tempting to believe he may have lied about his age – that he is, in fact, a well-preserved 40 in disguise. (Since everyone had to produce formal ID to verify their date of birth at the Birmingham auditions, this is not possible.) If Darius fails to make it into *Popstars* he could, perhaps, become a politician. Or – since it's impossible not to fall under the spell of those big brown eyes within the space of about 30 seconds – he could form a cult. So far, everyone has been seduced – so to speak – by him.

'I believe I can give and keep on giving,' he says. 'I've got talent, I know that. I want to realise my goal to be a fantastic entertainer, to reach a wide audience – that would be a dream come true.'

Darius has already considered the impact *Popstars* would have on his life. For one thing, he would have to drop out of university, where he is in his third year. For another, he would face separation from his family – including his much-loved little brother.

Part of the *Popstars* deal means sharing a house with the rest of the band, living in a location so secret that not even family and close friends will know the address. There is also the question of overnight fame.

All 33 are already beginning to consider the consequences of this.

'Nobody really knows for sure how they would cope,' Kym says. 'I can only say I feel I'm ready for it now. 'I've had all the rehearsals, been to the auditions, and now I'm ready for the real thing. I'm going to grab it with both hands if I get the chance.'

Darius believes he too is ready. 'I know the cameras will be in my face and that people will be knocking on my door wanting to know who I slept with last night,' he says. 'It doesn't worry me. I enjoy being faced with the kind of things most people would find intimidating.'

He has also considered the likely impact on his girlfriend of five months, Rachel. '*Popstars* is a big turning point. If the band were to take off ... it's very difficult,' he says.

And if he had to choose between the band and Rachel? He mulls this over. 'Without wishing to upset Rachel, the band. I feel hard saying that, but this has been a lifelong ambition. Rachel is the most important girl in my life, but I hope she would support me and be understanding.'

In the background, assistant producer Claire O'Donohoe checks her watch. Over the next three days there are more than 30 interviews to be done. Time is short and Darius has been chatting for more than half an hour. He could, one suspects, talk for Scotland. So far, we have merely scratched the surface. Reluctantly, we call it a day.

Less assured is Gary Lewis, 21, from the West Midlands. 'I can't believe I'm sitting here,' he says.

Six months earlier Gary was working full-time as a musician, playing duets with his then girlfriend in pubs and clubs. He gave it up to concentrate on hitting the big time. Now he has landed the biggest audition of his life.

'It's so nerve-racking,' he admits. 'I'm just giving it my best – and a bit more if I can. It's a funny atmosphere – trying to make friends, all that pressure.'

For Gary, the dancing is proving tougher than the singing. He's the first to admit he's not a natural mover. 'I'm probably the worst one here,' he says. 'The girls are brilliant and I'm there thinking, Oh, I can't get it...'

It's not just the dance steps that worry him. When he auditioned at Birmingham he hit it off with a girl called Hayley Evetts and the two started seeing each other. Hayley has also made it through to the last 33. The pair have now split up, but they are sharing a hotel room. Gary is keen to play down the relationship.

'We clicked and we started dating but it was casual,' he says. 'We're sharing a room but we're being very professional. It won't affect things in the slightest. We just had a little fling and it's over – neither of us are heartbroken.'

For Gary, making it to the final stage of the audition is already a dream come true. He was bullied at school and his self-confidence took a battering. He laughs now at the memory. 'I was ugly – I was spotty as well. In a way it was good. It's made me tougher.'

Gary wants to be a part of *Popstars* more than anything. 'I want to be in the band. I've tried lots of things in my life and it always comes back to music,' he says. 'I want to live the lifestyle. I want to perform. I want to play Wembley – that's my ultimate goal. I think God

Day One warm-up

The girls prove to be

better movers than some

of the boys.

has blessed me with these talents and I don't see why I should settle for second best – playing holiday camps or whatever – when I can have the big time, so I'll give it everything I've got.'

James Mason, from Kent, is slightly bemused at having made it to the final audition. James designs web sites and does removals – 'a bit different from all this.'

At the *Popstars* party the night before he had a lot to drink although, miraculously, claims to have no hangover. 'I just can't remember what I did last night. The drink was free and that's my downfall,' he says.

'If I don't make it through at least I can get completely drunk. If I do make it I'm Mr Serious.' He thinks for a moment. 'It's more likely I won't make it...'

He almost failed to make the second round of call-backs at Birmingham. Convinced he wouldn't get through anyway, he went out the night before and blew his train fare on a few drinks. Luckily, his step-brother, Dan, bailed him out and persuaded him to go.

'I've always had really low confidence and never believed I could get this far. I've always come second in everything I've done. It's nice to know I've made it to the last 33,' he says.

James, 21, the self-appointed practical joker in the pack, secretly unscrewed all the miniature pots of jam at breakfast that morning and dipped a finger in them. 'They'll hate me for that,' he says.

He admits to one concern at making it through to the band. 'Whenever I see myself on video I want to punch myself.'

Midway through Day One and Suzanne reckons she hasn't made the best start. 'I don't think I'm doing too well,' she admits. 'I did my solo before and felt I'd messed it up. I'm just trying to get my confidence up now. I'm singing a high harmony and I feel I'm too loud. I'm drowning every-body else out. I'm finding it hard to get the best out of my voice.'

It's not just her voice that's bothering her. Suzanne is also worried about her weight. She is convinced all the other girls in the room are much thinner.

'All my life I've had a weight problem,' she says. 'I put on weight at 14 and I've always been conscious of it, thinking, am I bulky? Do I look butch?'

Six months earlier she started working out at a gym. Just a couple of months ago she was a stone heavier. 'I've lost a lot of weight and I'm really proud,' she says. 'I'm starting to watch what I eat.' Chocolate and Chinese take-aways, however, remain a weakness.

'If I could get my figure how I want it I'd be fine,' she says. 'I don't think I'd ever stick my fingers down my throat or stop eating. I don't think it would get me down that much. I couldn't starve myself.'

At 19, Suzanne is already a seasoned performer. She was just three when she started dancing lessons, appeared in her first stage show – *Annie* – aged five, and racked up her TV debut in a show called *Elidor* at the age of 12.

For 18 months she has been playing the club circuit with an Abba tribute band.

While she admits the *Popstars* audition is tough, she remains optimistic. 'At the end of the day I'm not in this business to cry my eyes out after every audition,' she says. 'I'm in it to move on and get to the next one. I'm not a drama queen about it.'

Like all the others at Brixton, Suzanne has set her heart on being in the band. Sacrificing her privacy in the process is, she believes, a price worth paying.

'I don't know how I would cope, but I do want to be famous,' she says. 'I know that part of it is not having a private life.'

Realistically, she knows that fans love to get the lowdown on their favourite pop stars. Being splashed all over the tabloids goes with the territory.

'The press are interested in juicy gossip, just like this documentary series is,' she says. 'People won't be interested if you're not interesting, and it could do your career good if there's something juicy in the paper about you.'

As it turns out, Suzanne has nothing juicy to reveal (for now, at least). 'I'm a raving schizo,' she jokes. 'No, I've got a clean past – no criminal record or anything.'

Suzanne's pet hate is smelly feet. The idea of sharing a house does not faze her. 'I think I'll cope pretty well. I've experienced it with my current band. We do argue but that's only natural.'

Surprisingly, everyone at Brixton, claims to be happy at the prospect of moving in with four relative strangers.

'I think it's funny, I really do,' says Noel. 'You're really just going to have to work with whoever else is in the band. They'll be your new family and friends.'

He reckons he will be easy to live with. 'Oh yeah…as long as you don't' mind a bit of mess!'

Kym is also in favour. 'It will be great. You'll get to know each others' bad habits (she owns up to smelly feet) and probably there will be some terrible arguments, but show me a household that doesn't argue. I think the whole thing is quite exciting – like one big sleepover!'

Instant fame, nosy journalists digging around – nothing deters Suzanne.

'I'm happy to go along with anything to make me money and make me famous. At the end of the day I really love what I do.'

Frank Di Rollo, 23, from Edinburgh, admits he is finding Brixton tough.

'It's difficult in an environment like this to show your good points,' he says. 'You have 33 people in a room all competing for attention. In that situation I tend to sit back and withdraw.'

Ian Harvey, 22, from Southampton, found the early auditions nerve-wracking – 'singing to just three people – it's like a nightmare come true' – but is warming to Brixton.

'I'm feeling confident now, starting to enjoy it a lot more,' he says, grinning broadly.

Like most of the others, Ian is still suffering some nerves. Since his first audition he has started biting his nails. Just before Brixton he had sleepless nights. The enormity of it all is fast sinking in. 'This is the final part,' he says. I could get in – and if not I'm rubbing shoulders with the five people out there who will be the band.'

It's only within the past 12 months that he has started taking his singing seriously after entering a national karaoke contest – 'just for a laugh' – and, to his amazement, taking second place. 'I thought, Whoooaa! This is all right,' he said.

Ian has weighed up what it might mean to make it into the band. His biggest concern is his relationship with his girlfriend of 18 months. They live together, along with her two children aged five and six.

'She's a diamond lady,' he says. 'She knows I could be gone for months and not see her, but she's happy if I'm happy.'

The Green Mile

The waiting is the worst.

At 4p.m. on Day One everyone gathers for the dreaded Green Mile. Some curl up on the chairs that line the edges of the room – their first chance to sit down all day. Others sprawl on the floor. A game of cards is underway. Empty crisp packets and soft drink cans litter the floor. Myleene sits quietly. She appears undaunted by the prospect of the Green Mile. 'I have to think of this as a job,' she says. 'If I get hysterical

18

I can't do my job. Emotions are running high because we've all come so far, but it's just a case of bearing it out.'

At the far end of the main rehearsal room, Nigel Lythgoe, Paul Adam and Nicki Chapman sit in a row, pouring over files, preparing to give their verdict on the day's performance. It is not all good news. Cameras lock onto the door 10 metres away through which, one by one, the 33 will file to hear their fate. It is a long, tortuous walk. All anyone wants to know is that they have survived to Day Two. For five of the 33, their dream of being pop stars is about to be shattered.

As the Green Mile begins spirits are high. Within the space of a few minutes the mood has changed. Janis is shaking her head when she returns from her session with the judges. She is out. A mild shock wave ripples through the room. The chatter subsides and there is a moment of silence. Darius is the first to react. He throws his arms around her, dwarfing her tiny frame. The others applaud her. Janis, who has struggled to keep a brave face, crumples and disappears into the toilets with Sally.

'They didn't think I was right for a pop group,' she says, 'and to be honest, I'm not a pop person, so that's fine.' She wipes at her tears. 'I don't know why I'm crying. I'm happy with the decision. It's when you get too much sympathy it's upsetting. I was fine until Darius came over.'

Back in the waiting room, Ian, his hands over his face, lies on the floor under a sign that reads Quiet Please At All Times.

One by one, they face the judges. Suzanne returns with a thumbs up. She is through to the next day. Darius makes it too. Gary is also through. He flops to the floor in relief.

'I felt like if I can just get through the first day I can do the rest,' he says, visibly relieved. 'Bring it on!'

Ian has made it too. The first thing he does is phone his Mum to break the good news.

As tension mounts David walks the Green Mile. A camera tracks him all the way. How does he feel about the first day? He is cautiously optimistic. 'I think it went all right,' he says.

Kelli

Star quality but too

straight-faced?

Paul Adam confirms they are happy with his performance. 'We thought you sang well today,' he says. David is clearly relieved. He will be back in the morning.

Next up is Kelli. In previous auditions she has demontrated star quality. Day One at Brixton has thrown up some concerns, however. Her nerves have shown on her face. Kelli has got to smile more.

Nigel Lythgoe tells her she has a great voice and a great look. 'But if you don't smile it looks as if you're moody,' he tells her.

The judges still want to see her the next day. Kelli heaves a sigh of relief and gives them the smile they've looked for throughout the day before she leaves.

Warren is next and Nicki Chapman has some stern words for him. She wants to know if he feels it was wise to fly in from LA the day before. Warren, who has been battling with jet lag on top of a cold throughout the day, shakes his head. He begins to fear the worst, but the judges are not quite ready to let him go. They do want to shake up his attitude – for his own sake. Warren is convinced he has blown it. When Nicki finally advises him to get a good night's sleep ready for Day Two at Brixton he laughs in disbelief.

'Do you guys concoct ways to do this?' he wonders. As he leaves the room he lets out a noisy sigh of disbelief.

As the door clicks shut behind him Nicki Chapman also lets her guard down. 'I could not do that for any longer,' she admits.

Marc appears expecting bad news but the judges want to see him again. He is on the verge of tears when they break the news. 'Thank God for that!' he says.

Michelle is next. She is used to auditions having made it to the last 12 for the band Girl Thing. Despite her experience she appears nervous.

Quiet Please

Tension mounts as they wait

for the Green Mile.

'I thought this afternoon went a lot better than this morning,' she tells the panel.

'We'd like you to relax,' Nigel Lythgoe tells her.

Noel appears, the 'made in wales' logo on his tee shirt just visible beneath the black leather coat he now hugs about him.

'We're very pleased with you,' Nigel tells him. We don't want to change you.'

It is the news he wanted and as he leaves the room a whoop of delight goes up in the corridor outside. The judges laugh. 'Is there a camera outside the door?' says Nicki. 'If there isn't there'll be trouble,' Nigel replies.

Akiya, Sarah, TJ, Tony, Caroline, Hayley, Charlotte, Sally and Jessica are all invited back. Zahra faces the judges feeling less than confident. She has been unhappy with her performance that day and now she is wracked with nerves.

'My heart's beating fast,' she tells the panel.

Nigel Lythgoe is puzzled and disappointed. He knows that Zahra is capable of much more. 'I thought you were flat. The performance wasn't there today but in Birmingham you stood out,' he tells her.

Zahra is crestfallen. Paul Adam warns her it will get tougher with each day. Nigel wants to know where her sparkle has gone.

'I don't know. I've lost all my confidence,' she says.

Nigel reassures her. 'To be here you are just as good as they are. Come back tomorrow in a positive mood.'

When Louise faces the judges she learns at once she has survived Day One. Nigel Lythgoe has spotted an unfortunate trait in her performance, however. 'Be careful,' he tells her. 'You've got what I call the cabaret nod...' He demonstrates her habit – of which Louise is utterly unaware – of nodding at the end of each line of a song.

She takes the advice on board. As she leaves, Nigel grimaces. 'The cabaret nod...'

The judges are impressed with Kym. She looks good and her voice is strong. Even on the first day her qualities as a good all-rounder have shone through. Like the others, however, Kym is suffering an attack of nerves. 'I'm shaking,' she tells them. 'I'm more nervous now than ever.' Nicki tells her she is a great team player. Nigel believes she could improve the quality of her voice with singing lessons. All Kym wants to know is that she is through to Day Two. She leaves the room and calls home to break the good news to her parents in Wigan.

Frank is next and he is about to get some bad news. He has failed to deliver on the first day. There can be no second chance. Nicki tells him at once that it is the end of the line. While the judges are not looking for extroverts, Frank is just

too reserved. Paul urges him to work on his confidence. Nigel says he must learn to let his character shine.

Shar is also about to face disappointment. Again, the panel love her look, but she has been singing out of tune. She is taken aback. 'I thought I was singing too loud,' she says. In fact, there were times when she was barely audible.

James too has failed to win over the judges. He tells them, 'I don't think I did as well as everyone else.' Nigel noticed he struggled with the movement routines. 'You've got a good voice,' he says. 'And you're extremely good fun when you put your mind to it.'

Amanda too faces bad news. Somehow, she has not sparkled as much as at her previous auditions. 'We don't feel you're going to fit in the final group,' Paul explains.

The ecstasy and the agony

Danny's smile lights up the room, but it's all too much for Gary.

Kevin follows her in. He has made it to the next day. He has the right look and the right sound for *Popstars*. Already, he is establishing himself as an impressive contender. Taz too, has potential, but the panel fears he may be more suited to solo work. When he faces the judges Nigel Lythgoe sums up their disappointment.

'You're a great individual but we have to ask if you're right for a band,' he says.

Taz, hunched forward in his chair, blinks back tears. 'We know you can do better,' Nicki tells him.

They want him to work at blending in more with the others, rather than demonstrate his own vocal range at their expense.

'I'm confused. I need to know where I went wrong,' he says.

Nigel suggests he speak with Annie Skates, the vocal coach. All three judges want Taz to bring more concentration and discipline to his performance.

When he leaves Nigel turns to Paul and Nicki. 'The guys are far more emotional than the girls,' he says, surprised.

As Danny walks the Green Mile, his smile lights up the room. Throughout the first day he has proved outstanding in a quiet, unassuming way. The judges have no doubts about him.

'You've got a great vocal,' Nicki tells him. 'We'll see you tomorrow.' Danny grins.

'Keep that smile,' Nigel says. 'It brings a lot of warmth into the room.'

Paul is next and bounds up to the judges clutching his mobile phone. He is feeling confident. 'I got some good news during the day and that made me happy,' he says, arousing the curiosity of the panel.

Nigel prompts him. 'Good news – have you won the lottery?'

Paul appears thrown. He is not about to share his news.

His voice is good, but Nicki tells him he is getting lost in the crowd. He feels it is because there are too many people around him 'giving it large.'

'We don't need OTT characters,' Nigel says, 'but we do need people to shine. That's the only feedback I can give you. I can't tell you how to stand out.'

When Raymond appears Nigel praises his voice but raises doubts about his attitude. Already, Raymond has got on the wrong side of Annie, the vocal coach. It does not bode well. 'If you are to stand any chance of getting into this band your whole attitude has got to change,' Nigel says. 'When you're told to listen you *must* listen.'

Raymond explains that his throat is bothering him. In *Popstars*, illness is no excuse for poor performance or behaviour. Raymond is told to get a good night's rest and return in the morning.

Finally, Myleene faces the judges. The news that she has made it through to Day Two produces a huge smile. Later she confides that she has only brought three tee shirts with her in case her luck runs out mid week. 'If it doesn't I'll just have to do some washing,' she says.

DID YOU KNOW?

Myleene won a scholarship to do a post graduate course at the Royal Academy of Music in London when she was just 20. All the other students were at least ten years older than her.

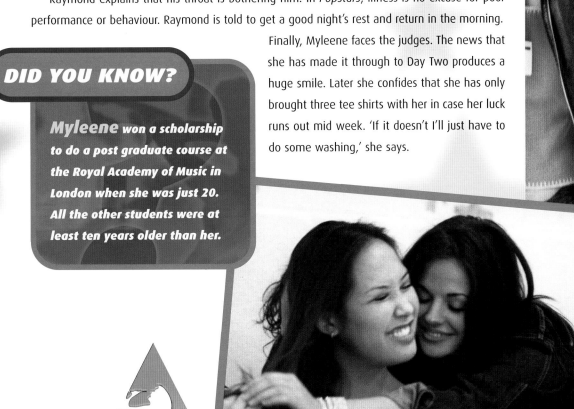

Day 2

Tuesday, 9.30a.m. The 28 survivors return to the rehearsal rooms for another intensive day of vocal work and choreography. All have had time to come to terms with losing friends the night before. All are acutely aware that only the best will survive the Green Mile at the end of the day.

'It is so hard to compete against people you've become attached to,' says Kym. 'You are competing against each other and you think, I love that person but I'm having to push myself forward in front of them. You've got to do it, but it's a lot harder than I thought, a lot tougher.'

'It's come to the crunch now,' says Hayley, 24, from Birmingham. The Green Mile the previous day was an ordeal for her. 'Once Janis was out the whole atmosphere changed and we all realised we could go in next and be told "No."'

On Day One Hayley felt her performance was not up to scratch. 'I was confident in my singing ability but I didn't perform well,' she said. 'I thought I'd be out yesterday so I'm grateful they've given me another chance. I've never felt like I did when I had to walk up to those judges.' She laughs. 'It was horrible.'

Like Gary, Hayley fears their short-lived fling might affect their chances of getting into the band. She is adamant what romance there was is over. 'We're just friends,' she says. 'It's like nothing ever happened. We're just two people who get on very well. We're really close and I think the world of him, but there's no relationship any more.'

She is, she says, happy being single. Men are a distraction. 'I haven't got time for a relationship. This is just me going for what I want to do.'

Popstars is the biggest audition Hayley has ever gone to, but she would prefer to know sooner than later if she is not going to make it. 'I'd rather go out today than go out on Thursday. I'd hate to get that close and not get it.'

Kelli, 18, also found the Green Mile daunting. 'It was hell. It was really nightmarish,' she says. 'The worst part was after you'd been told having to go back into the room and face everyone – "Did you get through? Did you get through?" I was dreading them telling me I hadn't made it and having to go back into that room...'

She concedes that the judges have a tough task. 'Talent-wise, I think the vocals are outstanding. If I was on the panel I wouldn't have a clue who to pick.'

Already, Danny is emerging as a star. His vocals are terrific and he possesses the star quality demanded by all the judges. Yet, on the face of it, Danny is an unlikely superstar. It is only three years since he began singing (on holiday in a karaoke bar in Tenerife). Auditions are new to him. Somehow, with apparent ease, he is shining. He has that indefinable something called presence.

'I have thought about fame,' he says. 'I suppose that's where people recognise you in the street, that kind of thing. I don't necessarily want to be famous. That's not what I'm looking for.

24

I want to be a successful singer; I know that goes hand in hand with fame.'

Unlike Danny, Charlotte, 19, has already learned to take auditions in her stride. 'I've been to lots and some I've got through, some I haven't. I auditioned for a girl band recently and got down to the last two – the last *two* – and didn't get it.'

At 25 David, from Gateshead, is the oldest in the group. He was 24 when he auditioned in Newcastle – right on the border of the upper age limit – and has since had a birthday. 'I do view this as a last chance for pop,' he says. 'I just want to see how far I can go.'

David was singing in a duet with his fiancée, Nicki, when he heard about *Popstars*. Both auditioned and made it as far as Birmingham. Now Nicki waits at home to see how far he'll progress.

In his past, David admits to being a bit of a lad. Not any more. 'I've finally screwed my head on properly,' he says.

Being in the band would not change a thing, he believes, although he admits Nicki is half dreading a call at the end of the week to say he's made it.

Michelle, too, is in a serious relationship. She is confident it would survive whatever the music industry threw her way. Michelle, 21, has come close to superstardom before – she made it to the last 12 for Girl Thing. Now she's giving *Popstars* her best shot.

She admits she is finding the whole process emotionally draining. 'I've cried all the way through this,' she says with a wry smile. 'I'm tearful at auditions whether I get turned away or accepted. I think I've got to toughen up a bit.'

Michelle has weighed up exactly what being in the band would mean. She is prepared to have her life scrutinised by the tabloids, to lose her privacy, to share a house with four people she hardly knows, and to cope with separation from her boyfriend, Matt.

'I want this so much,' she says. 'I'm not going to give up. I've done this for years and had really good feedback and really bad feedback. I've had a lots of knocks but I've never stayed down. I've always got up and carried on. I want this bad, real bad. I'll be disappointed if I don't get it, but I do realise they've got to get rid of people – not because they're not talented, but because they're not right for the band.'

By mid morning on Day Two Noel is irrepressible despite the mounting pressure. He seems totally unfazed by the Green Mile.

'I was fine,' he says. 'Everybody was like this...' he gnaws at his nails... 'and it was *ohmygod*...' He laughs. 'And I was unusually confident. The tension wasn't there for me like it was at Birmingham. I just felt so much more relaxed.'

Although Noel got good feedback from the judges, he is still treading carefully. 'It's a fine line between confidence and arrogance and I don't want to cross that. At the end of the day you have to go home and see your family and friends, who will watch you on the telly and go – "What were you *doing?*" You know?' He laughs. 'There are people back home you have to keep your feet on the ground for.'

He exudes confidence. 'I think I'm doing okay. I *hope* I'm doing okay with the performing, because that's what it's about at the end of the day.'

At the *Popstars* party a couple of nights earlier it was a different story. 'I was a bit uneasy,' he admits, 'trying to get to know everyone. I gave my Mum a bit of a naff phone call on Sunday saying, oh I'm not sure I want to do this... then, after yesterday it was like *yeah! Let's go!*'

Despite reservations about *Popstars* in the beginning, as Noel enters the final stages of the auditions, he has no doubts.

'I would *love* to be in the band. At the moment I'm working as a waiter and every day I go to work and think, what am I doing here? I would love to be able to put all this energy into something and say, "Look – here's me in a cheesey band!"'

In contrast to Noel, 21-year-old Akiya found the Green Mile traumatic. 'It was dire,' she says. 'I think I've started to realise now I have to enjoy it... but the tension and stress levels are exactly the same as yesterday because you're still thinking, it could be me today.'

The atmosphere in the audition hall is helping, however. 'Everyone realises they're in the same boat and that to get through they have to stick together. They're all very supportive,' she says.

Zahra, 18, from Plymouth, is struggling. On Day One her self-confidence plummeted. 'All these people are so pretty and talented I thought, I can't even compete with them, and I think that's what made me do not so well,' she says. 'I've been so self-conscious yesterday and today.'

Zahra, her shoulder-length hair in braids, is strikingly pretty. Ironically, it is her appearance that concerns her most.

'I've always had a thing with my weight since I was little,' she says. 'Once you start on that negative thing you find it with everything. So I'm going, "Oh, my voice isn't like theirs, I don't look like that..." once you get into that mood it's easy to stay there.'

She is aware that her performance must improve if she is to survive the second day.

Noel **sleepwalks. One night in the Popstars house Kym and Myleene watched him get up, go to the kitchen, make a drink and go back to bed – all without waking up!**

DID YOU KNOW?

'I think I'm still a little bit insecure, but I'm hoping I can stick it out.' She smiles through gritted teeth. 'I'm confident really.'

Warren, too, remains shaken by his encounter with the judges the previous day. 'Basically, it is real torture,' he says. 'And when you get in there and have to do the long walk to the judges it is petrifying.'

Day Two warm-up

The boys go for it!

The night before, Warren had an early night in the hope of shaking off his jet lag. Early into the second day of the audition, however, he suffered a setback. The song he had learned for his solo that day was not what the judges wanted. He felt like throwing in the towel.

'I'd learned a gospel song and they didn't want that. At the end of the day I sang well and they know I can sing...' he shakes his head...'if it's not good enough I did my best.'

Warren is a born-again Christian and believes his faith is guiding him. 'I genuinely feel inside that I was born to be a performer,' he says.

He is surprised at how keenly he is feeling the pressure, however. 'When we first started I saw a lot of people freaking out and I said, "No, that won't happen to me,"' he says. 'I didn't expect it to get to me to the point where I'd actually cry. It's overwhelming for me. I never dreamed I'd do that. I never thought I'd get this far.'

Marc, 18, never expected to do so well either. *Popstars* was his first audition. When he faced the judges at the end of Day One he thought he'd blown it.

'Nigel said he didn't think I'd done very well and I just sunk down in my chair and went bright red,' he says. 'I thought I was gone.'

Now he is suffering from a sore throat (a mini epidemic of sore throats has broken out) and is struggling with his voice.

'This morning we had to sing solos and I was really pushing it – I'm getting to the point where I'm losing my voice a bit,' he says. 'I'm disappointed with myself today because I know I can do better.'

Marc has already decided his future lies in music – whatever happens with *Popstars*. 'I love singing. The feeling I get is happiness. When you know you can hit that note, that's the most important thing – more than the money or the girls. If you enjoy it, it's going to show in your performance.'

Louise, 23, has been to several auditions, but none quite like *Popstars*. 'It's been more intense than any other audition,' she says. 'I feel more confident now and I'm enjoying it more, although having said that, there's a lot more pressure now because we're getting to the final stages.'

Louise has always wanted to be a performer. 'I've always known I have a gift,' she says. 'I know a lot of people can sing and dance, but I'm talking more a stage presence, something extra.'

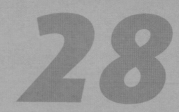

Louise must also work on losing the 'cabaret nod' Nigel Lythgoe warned her about at the end of Day One.

Caroline, 20, also has set her heart on a career in entertainment. Such is her dedication that every spare moment is spent rehearsing. 'I rehearse every single night and make sure I do an hour or two of singing,' she says. 'I go to dance classes, I went to stage school for two years. It's my life, basically.'

Like the others, she is finding the pressure more intense as the days go by. 'I've been nervous, I've been excited, I've been hopeful, not so hopeful. It's all a bit uncertain really. You think you're doing well but at the end of the day you're not sure what the judges are thinking or whether you're going to get through.'

Throughout the second day cameras continue to follow the would-be pop stars. There are no breaks, as such. Even lunch – a quick sandwich and a bar of chocolate for most – is filmed. All feel they are performing – and being assessed – even during the brief rest periods. They are right. The judges already know that everyone in the room has talent. They also want to get some sense of personality so that they can construct a band that is harmonious in every respect.

'There is a lot of pressure,' says Jessica. 'I do feel I'm being tested all the time – when I'm eating my sandwiches, when I'm in the hotel, not just when I'm singing and dancing. You can't ever completely relax because you know you're being watched and everything is being taken into account. It's so hard.'

Myleene is more tolerant of the cameras than many of the others. She accepts that they are an integral part of *Popstars*.

'There are going to be times when you want to step out of TV land and you're not going to get the opportunity to do so,' she says. 'At the same time it is the cameras that put you on screen in the first place.'

Kym agrees. 'I'm used to the cameras now,' she says. 'At the end of the day this is what I enjoy doing and the cameras are all part of that.'

At 4p.m. on Day Two the singing and dancing is over and the Green Mile beckons. As they wait, Gary paces about. His face is a picture of despair. 'If I don't get this I'm going to kill myself,' he says.

Ian admits that already the strain of the auditions is beginning to tell on his girlfriend at home in Southampton. The night before he phoned her and there were tears when she heard girls' voices in his room. 'There was nothing going on, but she's miles away and it's difficult for her,' he says.

One by one, they are called before the judges – in a different order to the previous day, which seems to throw them. First up is Myleene. She is through. Raymond, sitting on the floor with headphones on, is next. He is called three times before he hears his name over the sound of the music coming through his cans. He makes it too, but admits the process is fast becoming an ordeal. 'The pressure is getting more intense every day,' he says. 'Not a lot of us have been through this kind of pressure, and maybe if we don't make it we may decide never to go for another audition because it's too painful.'

Added to the pressure, Raymond is battling a cold, which is affecting his voice. He is taking painkillers every four hours to keep going.

Paul, Danny, Taz, Kevin, Akiya, TJ, Tony and Jessica make it. It all seems to be happening very fast compared with the night before. Marc declares that he is not feeling confident. 'If I get through I'm going to drink lots of water tonight and go to bed early. I think I got to bed too late last night and this morning my voice sounded dreadful.'

Kym is called and a whoop of encouragement goes up in the room. Moments later she is back yelling, 'Yes, yes, yes!'

Darius is anxious. He feels he may have angered the judges by messing about when it came to performing his solo earlier on in the day. Nigel Lythgoe had intervened, unamused. 'I should have just got on with it,' Darius admits.

Kym, meanwhile, is on the phone to her Mum to break the good news. 'I'm through!' she tells her. 'She's crying now,' she says. 'Don't cry – now you're making me cry.' She puts a hand over her eyes.

Gary is flat out on the floor with his hands over his eyes. Darius sits alone staring out of the window, apparently giving himself a pep talk.

Meanwhile, Louise returns from the judges shaking her head. She is out. Kym can barely believe it. 'Why, why? Oh, baby.'

Caroline appears. She too is on her way home. Earlier in the day she had spoken about the possibility of rejection, saying, 'If I don't get this there is no point in moping around. If they give me criticism, I have to take that and move onto the next audition. I'm certain this is what I want to do, and I'll just carry on.'

Louise is also determined to maintain a brave face. 'It's all right. I know I hit a wrong note,' she says. 'They were really nice to me.'

Michelle stares at Louise and Caroline, stunned. 'I can't believe it,' she says. 'Two of the least likely people to go...'

Louise smiles broadly at the camera just a few inches from her face. 'Go away,' she says good-naturedly.

Caroline is on her mobile phone. 'I'm coming home,' she says.

Zahra appears. She shakes her head, tearful. Noel, who has struck up a close friendship with her, puts his arms round her.

'I don't know why I'm crying,' she says. 'I'm really embarrassed.' She gazes at the camera. 'What can I say? Sorry, Dad.'

Noel is shocked. 'We've been together since Cardiff,' he says, unable to believe that Zahra is out. 'When you spend time like this with people you form the kind of close relationships that would normally take months.'

Despite her own success, Kym is also tearful. 'This is horrible, losing people. I really don't like it.' She rubs her bare arms. 'I've got goosepimples.'

Gary has disappeared. When he returns all eyes are on him. He shakes his head. 'No, no, I've not been in yet. I've just been to the toilet...'

Michelle, Hayley, Sarah and Warren are all through. Marc's worst fears are realised. His suspicions about his poor performance that day are confirmed when he faces the judges. He fights back tears when he tells the others he is out. 'It's the end of the audition but it's not the end of the world,' he says. Marc has already made up his mind to try and get a place at stage school. 'This was my first audition,' he says. 'I've been told I've done well to get this far.'

Noel has made it. Kelli is also through. Taz wanders about the room shaking his head. 'All this again tomorrow, man,' he mutters. 'The same again tomorrow.'

Charlotte is out. 'It's okay,' she tells the others. 'Please don't feel sorry for me.'

Darius steps forward and hugs her. 'Guys – a big hand for Charlie.'

Charlotte is buoyant. 'I can go home and sleep in my own bed tonight!'

To Taz's delight, David – his room mate – is through. 'My mentor,' Taz declares, hugging him. 'He got me through today.'

Ian is now pacing about waiting to be called. 'Oh my God,' he says, when his name is called. Seconds later he is back, delighted. 'All they said was, "We'll see you tomorrow – and get some sleep." I didn't even get to sit down!' He shakes his head in disbelief. 'I didn't even get halfway across the room...!'

Ian, who admits he has perhaps been too much the life and soul of the party so far, is determined to take the judges advice. 'I really want to get in this band, so if they say go to bed early, I'm going,' he says, before heading off to tell his Mum the good news.

Gary goes to face the judges. His hands are raised in triumph when he returns. 'They told me they didn't want to see me stopping up late, getting drunk. They want me to get to bed and get some sleep.'

David points at Ian. 'So, basically, stay away from him!'

Suzanne and Sally are both through.

Darius is the last to see the judges. Minutes tick by. 'Is Darius still in there?' says David. 'He seems to have been in a long time.'

Darius is facing bad news. The judges are telling him he is out. Typically, he challenges their decision, thereby prolonging the process.

Finally, he reappears. It is not immediately clear whether he is in or out. He holds up a hand to silence the room. 'Hey guys, I just want to thank you so much for all your smiles and support and hugs and to wish you all the best...'

Kym, Sally, TJ and Michelle are in tears, although Darius is composed. 'I don't want sympathy from anyone here,' he tells them. 'We're all talented people and we're all going to make it one day.'

Out but not down

It's not the end of the world

for Charlotte (top) or Marc.

Michelle can barely believe it. Some of the people she has become closest too have gone on the same day. Like many of the others, she never expected Darius to go.

'He's like everyone's big brother and for me one of the most talented boys here. I don't know why they're letting him go. I can't believe it. He's been everybody's best friend and kept everyone going.'

If Darius is sad to go, he is covering his disappointment well. He remains defiant in defeat.

'I am going to be one of the best singer-songwriters that Britain has ever seen. I'm going to have a Number One single by the age of 26 and before the age of 30 I'm going to have a triple platinum album,' he says.

The previous day Darius had spoken passionately about his desire to be in a band. Now he accepts he is more suited to a solo career.

'Perhaps I will do better as a solo performer,' he says. 'I'm going to improve myself and I'm going to re-emerge. My time, my big break, my re-birth will happen. It's just a question of when.'

There is no doubt that Darius has made a huge impact on the group. 'I've got to nurture the gifts that God has given me,' he says. 'I've been given a voice, I've been given a presence, I've been given the ability to affect people, and I really have to work on that.'

As Darius leaves and prepares to return to Scotland no one really believes that they have seen the last of him.

'I don't believe other people could have worked with him but I do believe the talent was there,' Nigel Lythgoe says later. 'He was too tall for the band and whether he was feeding his ego by embracing everyone, I don't know. I would have thought so. I liked him but I'm afraid I would have to keep telling him to shut up and calm down.'

Nigel admits to being mistrustful of Darius's motives. 'At the end of the day he was extremely manipulative and brilliantly so. He always knew that whatever happened he had seeded enough in each programme to be there. He was extremely clever.'

Darius departs...

but leaves behind some well-chosen words for the remaining pop stars.

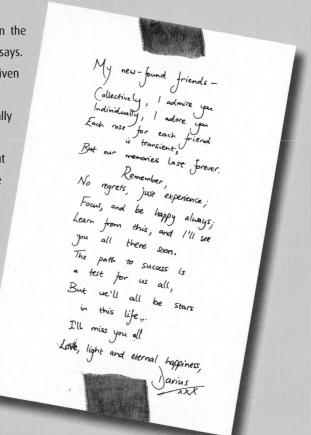

My new-found friends —
Collectively, I admire you
Individually, I adore you
Each rose for each friend
    is transient,
But our memories last forever.
    Remember,
No regrets, just experience;
Focus, and be happy always;
Learn from this, and I'll see
you all there soon.
The path to success is
a test for us all,
But we'll all be stars
    in this life,..
I'll miss you all
Love, light and eternal happiness,
          Darius
            xxx

32

Shortly after 9a.m. on Wednesday, the remaining 22 arrive at the rehearsal rooms. The atmosphere is subdued. Everyone is talking about Darius's departure. The night before he had gathered everyone and sung to them (a song hurriedly composed for the occasion). It reduced the entire group to tears.

Some had chosen not to be there, among them Sarah. 'I believe it was beautiful but I didn't want to be there,' she says. 'I'd already had a good cry and I needed to concentrate on getting through today.'

She is suffering from a cold, and she's not the only one. There seems to be an outbreak of minor ailments among the group.

'You can feel a change in the atmosphere this morning,' she says. 'There are still positive vibes going round, but...'

Day Three marks a departure from the first two days. The group is being rested from the intense singing and dancing of the early part of the week. Instead, they arrive to find Conrad Potts, a corporate training consultant, waiting for them. He is about to put them through their paces with a series of tests designed to reveal whether or not they are team players. The exercises will also help the group bond.

It was Nigel Lythgoe's idea to bring in the training guru. 'They had gone through a rigorous confidence-sapping exercise and there had been a lot of fear and anxiety,' says Conrad Potts. 'What they needed was a day when they could work together and support each other as a team because eventually five of them would have to do just that.'

The session also served to distract the group from the main topic of conversation – Darius. He might have gone, but his presence weighed heavy in the air.

Kym admits that the first two days have been mentally exhausting. Despite going to bed early, she could not sleep. By far the toughest part has been saying goodbye to the people she has become close to.

'Darius was like everyone's big brother,' she says, echoing Michelle. 'People went to him for advice and encouragement and cuddles. He was like the big protector. Nobody believed he'd be, like, you know – got rid of...'

'I think Darius was like a bit of glue that held everybody together,' says Jessica. 'I think he was a good support for everybody in his own way. We have lost 11 people now. We all realised last night how serious the whole thing is.'

TJ, who had wept over Darius the night before, was also struggling to come to terms with his departure. Like so many of the others, she had imagined he was a dead cert for the band.

'I was shocked,' she says. 'I knew how much he wanted it and I just felt so sad for him.'

TJ has already had a taste of the pop industry. A former dancer, she joined Eternal when Kelle left. It was not a happy experience and she is loathe to rake over the details again now.

'I spent ten months auditioning, flew out to LA, did a photo shoot, then just had to come home.' She shakes her head. 'I just quit... after five days.'

She is reluctant to say more. 'It was just a gradual build-up. I hate talking about this. I would hate the girls to think I was bitching about them,' she says, covering her face with her hands. 'I just want to leave it *so* behind me. After this I am *never* going to talk about it again.'

TJ had vowed to turn her back on the music business two years earlier, following her experience with Eternal. It was thanks to her younger sister that she auditioned for *Popstars*.

'It's a very scary industry and I've built a little barrier round myself now,' she says. 'I'm not fazed any more. If I did make it I'd be very clear about that. When I'm working I'll do my job 100 per cent. When I'm not working I'll demand my privacy.'

Unlike some of the girls at the final auditions who have expressed concerns about being overweight, TJ – tiny, lithe and muscular – has no such complaints.

'I used to be so ashamed of this body when I was younger 'cause everyone used to think I was a man,' she laughs, glancing at her toned arms. 'Now it's "in" to look like this, so I'm okay... but when it becomes fashionable to be a bit feminine again I'm in trouble 'cause I look like an adolescent boy!'

Like TJ, Tony is also a dancer. Having toured with Michael Flatley's *Lord Of The Dance,* he is used to performing to a rigorous schedule before huge audiences. Still, he finds *Popstars* tough.

'I think they're putting us through the most gruelling process imaginable to see how we come out the other side,' he says. After a moment's thought, he adds, '*If* we come out the other side.'

Tony has spent a lot of time over the first two days thinking hard about what the judges might be looking for in the final line-up for the band – and wondering if he fits the bill.

'They have a very definite idea of what they want and I have a definite idea of who I am, what I am, and whether I want to fit into their idea of a band,' he says. 'There's a bit of a conflict at times.'

DID YOU KNOW?

Suzanne used to sing with a band called The Right Stuff. They played clubs and ferries too. 'It was really hard work. We'd do five 45-minute sets a day,' she says.

All of the remaining 22 have a clear idea of who they are. No one wants to bend their personality to fit what they imagine to be the judges' criteria.

Danny, 21, is determined, above all, to be himself. 'That is really so important to me,' he says. 'If I can't be myself then I can't be anything else.'

In the space of two days Danny has established himself as one of the most laid-back members of the group. He doesn't seek attention but still manages to shine. Not only is his voice outstanding but he also has the kind of 1,000 watt smile you just can't miss.

Danny has no intention of playing to the cameras. 'In situations like this your true self comes out,' he says. 'It's a 24/7 feeling at the end of the day. When you're out bowling or eating your meal the camera is *always* there. If you're going to be hyperactive you've got to keep that up all the time.'

Like Noel, Danny knows his friends and family will be watching *Popstars*. That is enough to keep his feet firmly on the ground.

'If I'm not myself they're going to look at me and think that's actually not the person they know, and I'd find that quite difficult,' he says. 'So I have to stay myself.'

For Danny, every day at Brixton is a bonus. 'I just think, I'm through to the next day, and that's really good.' He smiles. 'D'you know what I mean?'

Myleene too is taking nothing for granted. She is down to her last tee shirt. All being well, she will be doing some hand washing later that night in her hotel room. 'I didn't want to pack for the week because I knew there was a chance I wouldn't be here all week,' she says.

Like Danny, she has approached the auditions in her own style, determined to be true to herself at all times. A talented musician, she plays piano, harp and violin. Vocally, she is outstanding.

So far, she has been impressed with the *Popstars* process. 'It's the genuine article,' she says. 'The cameras are there, they're seeing if you can sing, if you interact with people, if you can react under pressure. I think those are the right credentials to make a successful band and I want to be part of it.'

Paul, 18, also likes what he sees at the auditions. 'I just look round the room and everyone is so talented, so good,' he says. 'They want to give five good people a chance and I want to be part of that.'

Paul has wanted to perform for as long as he can remember. Making it into the band would fulfill a lifetime ambition. 'It would be a dream come true. I can't describe how it would make me feel. It's everything. That's what I want to do in life.'

Taz, 19, has found the auditions emotionally draining. Day by day, the pressure becomes greater.

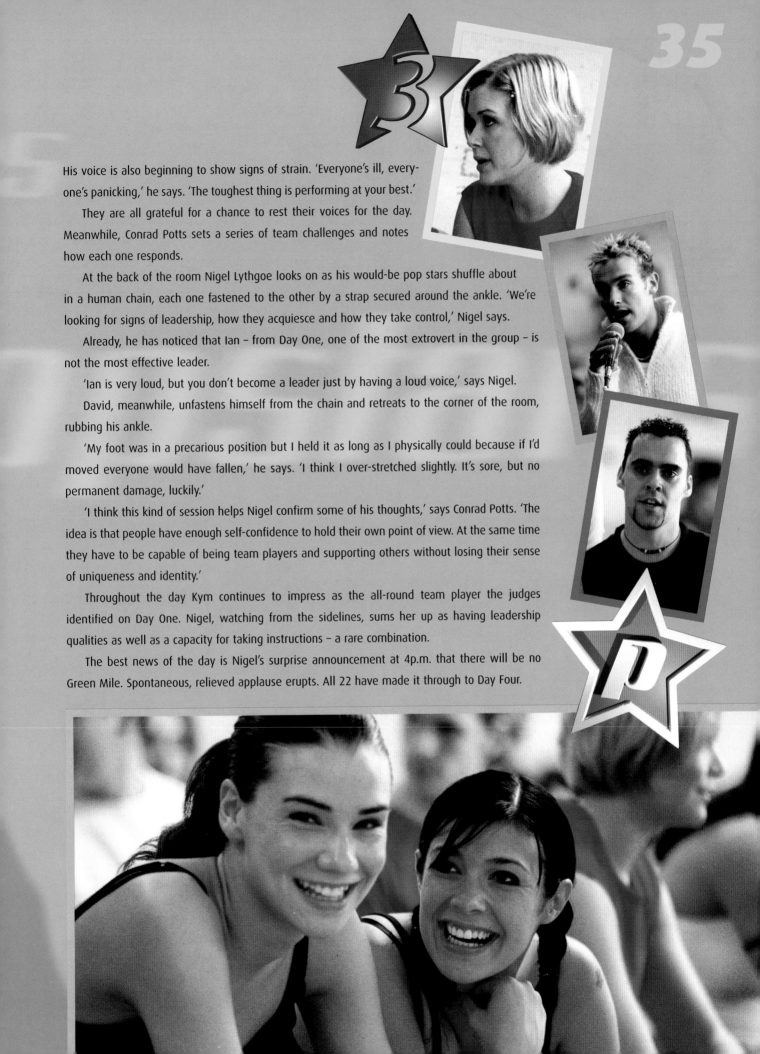

His voice is also beginning to show signs of strain. 'Everyone's ill, everyone's panicking,' he says. 'The toughest thing is performing at your best.'

They are all grateful for a chance to rest their voices for the day. Meanwhile, Conrad Potts sets a series of team challenges and notes how each one responds.

At the back of the room Nigel Lythgoe looks on as his would-be pop stars shuffle about in a human chain, each one fastened to the other by a strap secured around the ankle. 'We're looking for signs of leadership, how they acquiesce and how they take control,' Nigel says.

Already, he has noticed that Ian – from Day One, one of the most extrovert in the group – is not the most effective leader.

'Ian is very loud, but you don't become a leader just by having a loud voice,' says Nigel.

David, meanwhile, unfastens himself from the chain and retreats to the corner of the room, rubbing his ankle.

'My foot was in a precarious position but I held it as long as I physically could because if I'd moved everyone would have fallen,' he says. 'I think I over-stretched slightly. It's sore, but no permanent damage, luckily.'

'I think this kind of session helps Nigel confirm some of his thoughts,' says Conrad Potts. 'The idea is that people have enough self-confidence to hold their own point of view. At the same time they have to be capable of being team players and supporting others without losing their sense of uniqueness and identity.'

Throughout the day Kym continues to impress as the all-round team player the judges identified on Day One. Nigel, watching from the sidelines, sums her up as having leadership qualities as well as a capacity for taking instructions – a rare combination.

The best news of the day is Nigel's surprise announcement at 4p.m. that there will be no Green Mile. Spontaneous, relieved applause erupts. All 22 have made it through to Day Four.

Thursday at 9.20a.m., and the 22 return to the rehearsal rooms in high spirits. Some are clutching a single red rose, a gift from Darius. The flowers arrived that morning along with a letter, 'To be opened and read to my friends, as a group, whether they get through today or not.' On the way to the rehearsal rooms Noel, in his best Scottish accent, has read it aloud.

Suzanne confesses she is more nervous with each passing day. Myleene does the splits, making it look effortless. Akiya has a go and gives up with a shriek of pain. Taz, in dark glasses, a CD player in his hand, dances in the middle of the room, seemingly lost in his own world.

Tony, cross-legged on the floor, says his healthy eating habits – carefully observed for the two weeks leading to the auditions – have rapidly gone out the window. 'I've been eating really well,' he says. 'Six portions of fruit and six portions of veg a day. Now with all these crisps and chocolate I'm coming out in spots...'

David has shaved off his beard at Nigel's request. 'David is the oldest one in the group,' Nigel says. 'I just wanted to see if he looked younger without the beard.'

Several are nursing minor ailments. Sarah has had a nosebleed. Ian's throat is raw and he is having difficulty breathing. He wants to see the nurse.

Nigel Lythgoe stands at the front of the room and demonstrates the warm-up steps to loud applause. Noel, meanwhile, is bandaging up his knee. Having dislocated it twice before he is not about to take any chances.

They split into groups to work on harmonies with vocal coach Annie Skates, and movement with choreographer Di Cook. The afternoon has been set aside for what Nigel Lythgoe calls 'games,' when they will all in turn face the media at a series of mock press conferences.

'You'll face the press as if you've just had a Number One single,' he says. 'And we will have members of the press there.' In fact, most of the questions will come from Polydor's Artist Development Manager Peter Loraine (credited as the man who first dubbed the Spice Girls Posh, Scary, Baby, Sporty and Ginger) and James Herring, who runs a Public Relations company.

Nigel knows this will be the toughest day. A few hours later the judges will be breaking bad news to eight of the 22. 'Our job is going to be terrible at the end of the day, but now when we say to people, I'm sorry, they're still going to be happy with the week they've had, and that's pleasing,' he says.

'You're not breaking hearts. That's the tough thing, when you break hearts – and that's got to be done sometimes.' A few hours later he will be eating his words.

Throughout the morning Annie Skates gets to grips with their harmonies, having divided the 22 into groups, depending on their range. As they run through the old Simon and Garfunkel classic, Bridge Over Troubled Water, phrase by phrase, Annie corrects them repeatedly. 'Much as I love pub singing I don't think it's appropriate here,' she tells the boys. 'It's a gentle ballad.'

Now that the group is down to 22 Annie is happy with the overall standard. 'I've told them if I was booking them as professional singers I wouldn't let them get away with anything, so I won't let them in this instance either,' she says. 'I am giving them praise where due, but they need to learn and they need to know what the standard is, so I am being tough with them.'

Annie has noticed that some are growing in confidence as the week has gone on, while others react less well to the pressure. 'I can see that some people are really coming out of themselves and starting to blossom, while some are getting more nervous the further they get,' she says.

She has noticed that Ian's voice is beginning to show signs of strain. 'He is struggling,' she says. 'His voice is still there, it's a very good voice, but I can tell he's having problems. He is finding it hard to reach notes that normally are not a problem, but I don't think it's getting in his way. It's still coming through.'

Annie has a few thoughts on who should make it into the band. 'I really like Suzanne and Kelli, but it would have to be one or the other because they both sing the same part. Myleene is very strong and Kym is also very good.' She admits she is glad she is not making the decision. 'I think I'd find it really tough,' she says.

Ian, meanwhile, has gone missing. He is with Nurse Yasmin Appleby complaining of a sore throat and breathing problems. His face is waxen. There are dark shadows under his eyes. 'I woke up sweating this morning and coughed and coughed and couldn't stop,' he says. 'I panicked as well, I suppose I got nervous. I thought, I'm ill – I'm going to blow it. My blood pressure shot up to something stupid and I had a panic attack.'

Yasmin dispenses a spoonful of black, evil-looking medicine. Ian is doubtful. 'What's it taste like?' he says.

'It's good,' she assures him.

He swallows and pulls a face. 'You absolute liar!' he says.

Ian fears that he is missing a crucial part of the audition. 'I just want to go in and watch, see what's going on,' he says.

Yasmin gives him a powerful lozenge to sooth his throat. In 20 minutes or so, he should start to feel better. His cough will return, she warns, once he starts singing.

He rejoins the group, insisting he is well enough to sing. But after a few lines he admits to feeling the strain. 'I'm just glad it's a soft song that doesn't need a lot of power,' he says. 'I was out of breath on almost every note.'

Yasmin Appleby is being kept busy with a stream of complaints. There are five sore throats. One girl has a kidney infection. Another has a mild ankle sprain. Raymond tells Yasmin his throat is still bothering him. Worse, three of his wisdom teeth have started to ache.

David is among those who have requested something for his throat, but remains positive. 'If I go out today I'll probably shed some tears,' he says. 'Yesterday was a big bonding session and I'll be sad to leave, but if I do go then at least I've had a fantastic few days.'

By lunchtime – which everyone works through – Ian seems back to his usual, bubbly self. It is, however, an act. He admits he still feels awful. 'You can only do your best,' he says. 'I'm just not letting it show.'

Nigel Lythgoe is not surprised at the outbreak of illness among the group. 'They're probably using their voices more than they ever have before,' he says. 'Until they train their voices properly they will get sore throats. I'm not sure with Ian... he's really got a closed-up chest, and that's far more than just a sore throat.'

After lunch, John Kennedy, chairman and chief executive of Universal Music Group – Polydor's parent company – arrives. Nigel gets the group to perform Bridge Over Troubled Water to a backing track, plus an a cappella number they have been rehearsing. Kennedy applauds loudly.

It's mid afternoon and the first of the mock press conferences is about to begin. Michelle, Sally, Taz, Kevin and Kelli are the first to face the press as a 'band.' They field a barrage of questions about how they get along, whether they're in a relationship, how they're going to spend their money, their views on other bands. Kevin admits he is not a fan of S Club 7. He is cautioned about this later. 'You really need to be careful what you say about other bands – you might have to appear on *Live and Kicking* with S Club 7,' PR supremo James Herring tells him.

Face the press

Myleene and Raymond field

some difficult questions.

They leave the room under strict instructions not to give anything away to the others waiting outside. The next 'band' troops in – Myleene, Kym, Raymond, Hayley and Akiya.

Kym is asked whether she has a boyfriend. 'Not any more,' she says. What if he sells his story? Kym laughs. 'He's not got much to tell.'

One of the reporters puts Myleene on the spot. What does she think about the legalisation of cannabis? 'If I knew more about it I'd feel comfortable commenting. Until then, I'd rather not say,' she says.

John Kennedy smiles. 'Perfect answer,' he murmurs.

Another asks Kym if she would pose topless. 'No,' she says. What about people who do? Kym shrugs. 'That's up to them.'

As for her tattoos – Kym has one on her arm (the Chinese symbol meaning woman) and another on her bottom (a panther) – what if 14-year-old fans copy her? 'That's the tattoist's fault,' she says firmly. 'If someone over 18 wants one that's fine.'

Once it's over the journalists give their verdict. They love Kym. 'She's a leader, very switched on,' says one. Myleene is also singled out for praise.

'Very good, very confident.' Her answer on the cannabis question was exactly right.

The third 'band' – Tony, Gary, Sarah, Jessica and Warren – steps forward. Tony is quizzed about Steps. Is he a fan? 'I have three of their albums,' he says. And his favourite track on the new album? 'Stomp,' he replies.

The reporters want to know what he thinks of Michael Flatley. Is he difficult to work for? 'He is amazing. That's why I'm here today,' says Tony, refusing to be drawn.

The question of drugs comes up. Jessica, who has vowed to be truthful at all times, admits to having smoked cannabis. She appears unrepentant. It is a mistake. The journalists seize on it. 'You're a role model,' one tells her.

'I've been through it and chosen to leave it behind,' she replies.

Tony attempts to rescue her. 'There is no one who has not made mistakes,' he says.

Afterwards, Peter Loraine, Artist Development Manager at Polydor, tells Jessica her drugs revelation would have got her onto every front page. 'You'd be reported as saying you approve of teenagers taking drugs.'

'You didn't show any remorse,' says James Herring. 'A press conference is not a job interview. It's fine to say no comment.'

Jessica is distraught as she leaves. Privately, the judges praise Tony. 'We gave him a hard time but he handled it,' says Peter Loraine.

James Herring says Jessica's disclosures would have caused chaos had it been a real press conference. 'They had a much bigger story to talk about – their Number One single,' he says. 'But once one person puts up their hand and says they've taken drugs that trashes the whole thing.'

Next up are Danny, Noel, Paul and TJ. Noel is asked what it was like working on Ibiza. 'I wasn't near the mad part of the island,' he says. Ever taken drugs, Noel? 'No.'

How will you spend you first million? His family and friends will come first. His cousin, Luke, who is seriously ill with cancer, is top of his priorities. 'It would be nice to give him whatever he wants,' he says. 'The Ferrari can wait.'

TJ, who once posed topless, is quizzed about the picture. 'I am not even slightly worried about it,' she says, although her parents don't know about it.

Danny is asked what he thinks of Five. 'They're a good group,' he says.

Peter Loraine from Polydor puts them on the spot. 'Have any of you lied during this press conference?'

'Have *you*?' retorts TJ, laughing.

Staying cool

Danny and Noel win over the press.

39

The journalists are impressed. They have met their match. 'You were very good on the topless picture,' Peter Loraine tells her.

'I can't wait to see the photograph,' Nigel Lythgoe tells her.

'You'll have to find it first!' she says.

'Don't worry, I will!' Nigel assures her.

When the band leaves the journalists rave about Noel. Danny's smile has captivated them. Nigel agrees. 'He does light up the room.'

Finally, Suzanne, David and Ian face the press. The journalists want to know if Suzanne would ever pose naked. She shrugs. 'Depends how much money was in it...' She laughs. 'Probably not.'

Is she a good role model? 'Yes. I don't smoke, no drugs, and I don't like drinking,' she tells them.

The journalists quiz David about his fiancée. They wonder how he would react if Kylie suggested a cosy drink together at the trendy Met Bar. David is firm. If there was even a hint of hanky panky he would decline. His answer prompts snorts of disbelief.

Another turns to Suzanne. Ant or Dec? She considers for a second. 'Ant,' she says, grinning.

Once they leave, the journalists give their verdict on Suzanne. 'She's brilliant, very bubbly, not scared by anything,' says James Herring.

David's comment on Kylie has left Peter Loraine incredulous. 'Would you go out with Kylie? *No. I find that very unlikely,*' he says.

By 5.30p.m. the press conferences are over, the room is cleared, and the judges prepare for the Green Mile.

Day Four

The tears start before they even face the judges.

The 22 slump in heaps in the waiting room. Noel is telling TJ to watch the film, *The Green Mile*. 'You must see it then all this will make sense,' he says. 'Death row and all that.'

He pulls a soft toy from his pocket, a mascot given to him by Zahra. 'This is Crumpet,' he says.

Nearby, Danny tucks into a bar of chocolate. 'This is the first thing I've eaten today,' he says. 'Normally I eat around midday, but I didn't get round to it. Too much going on.'

Jessica is worried that her performance at the press conference will have gone against her, although the judges have already said it is not a factor. Still, she is anxious.

'I feel quite upset about it. I said I would always be honest and I have been and now I've learned – not that dishonesty is the best policy – but just to be more careful.'

Noel and TJ are also swapping notes on the press conference. 'I was getting more nervous as we were waiting to go in because the others were coming out and weren't allowed to say anything,' Noel says.

He laughs at the suggestion he enjoyed it. 'I tried to look

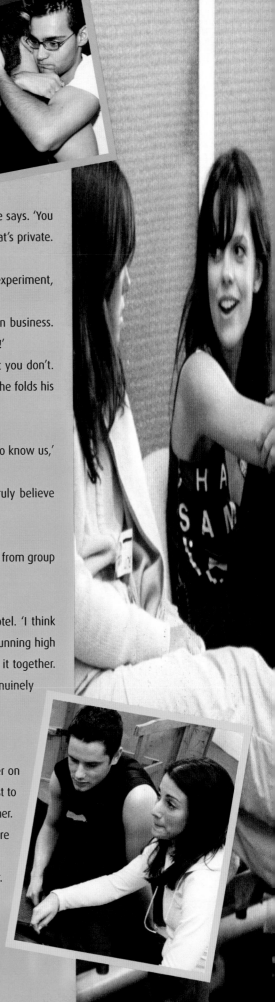

like I enjoyed it. I wanted to come across as confident. You're going to find situations you're not entirely comfortable with and you just have to deal with them, 'cause they're all part and parcel of the business.'

TJ, who was wary of facing the press, admitted she revelled in the experience. 'I used to think it would be really scary but journalists are just people,' she says. 'You just have to give it your best and you can say, "No – I'm not going to answer that. That's private. Mind your own business."' She laughs.

Noel reckons it will get easier with practise. 'It's like being part of a big social experiment, going through all this,' he says. 'Sociologists would have a field day watching us all!'

TJ is warming to the idea of being able to tell nosey reporters to mind their own business. 'Now I know,' she says. 'When people tell their life stories it's by choice. I'm appalled!'

Noel agrees. 'I always had the impression that bands had to give everything, but you don't. You don't have to say anything if you don't feel like it. You can just sit there and go...' he folds his arms and gazes into the distance.

The pair then discuss how the press conference will be edited for television.

'If we're edited properly then people can get to know us, and they will feel they do know us,' TJ says.

Noel is convinced that Darius will emerge as the 'Nasty Nick' of the series. 'I truly believe that,' he says.

TJ shakes her head. 'Someone told me his spirit lives on...'

'The way he has gone about everything has been very clever,' says Noel. 'He went from group to group to group – I never knew where I stood with him. I was like...' He shrugs.

'I cried for him when he went out – I really meant it as well,' TJ says.

Noel had watched Darius perform his farewell song two nights earlier at the hotel. 'I think when people cried it wasn't about Darius leaving, it was more to do with emotions running high throughout the day,' he says. 'Everybody had lost a friend and we'd all been through it together. The stress gets to a certain level and something has to give. Some people were genuinely upset that Darius was going, but others were just upset.'

'He is so young, just 20,' TJ says.

'He is a very, very clever man,' Noel says.

Suddenly, the Green Mile is underway and Sally is called first. The others cheer her on as she goes to hear her fate. Moments later she is back shaking her head. Sally is the first to go out. Kym jumps up and hugs her. 'I'm all right,' she tells the others. They all applaud her.

David is anxious but refuses to give way to his nerves. 'I'm not going in there thinking I'm going to fail, because if I do then I will,' he says.

Gary goes in next. Kym slumps into her seat. Sally's departure has unsettled her. 'That's me gone as well,' she says. 'That's me on death row too, I'm telling you.'

Gary returns and punches the air. 'Yes!' They all cheer.

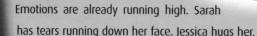

Emotions are already running high. Sarah has tears running down her face. Jessica hugs her.

Kym is worried. 'I'm going to get kicked out,' she tells Taz.

'Did you do your best today? That's all that matters,' he says.

Jessica is gloomy. 'I did my best and my worst,' she says.

Suzanne has gone to face the judges. 'If she's not in I will eat my knickers,' declares Kym, adding, 'As long as they're not dirty ones...' She clamps a hand over her mouth, horrified. 'Oh – only I could say a thing like that!'

Suzanne returns smiling. She has made it. Jessica rushes up and flings her arms round her. Ian too, despite the problems that have plagued him all day, is through. He drops to the floor and covers his face with his hands. 'I can't believe it,' he says. 'I'm just so happy – I live to fight the last day!' He laughs, relieved and vows to have an early night to give his voice a chance to recover. 'My voice is still there,' he says. 'It was just hiding away a bit today. You watch – mentally I'm back on top.'

David, who has also been nursing a sore throat, is through too. It is the end of the line for Hayley, though. She returns to face the group in tears. Kym wraps her arms round her.

'It's very sad. I've only been here four days but it feels like I've spent months with these people,' Hayley says. 'They can't really give you a reason for having to go. They just say you're not right for the band. But they've given me that push to keep going, and I will now.'

Kelli and Michelle are both through to the final day. Noel has made it too. He bursts into the room, delighted. 'What's Noel doing tomorrow? *Coming back!*' A cheer goes up.

Warren, however, is out. The room falls silent. He stands for a moment fighting back tears. 'The only reason I'm crying is because I'm really going to miss you guys,' he tells them.

TJ and Tony are in. Akiya and Sarah are out. Sarah is tearful but remains positive. 'I've really enjoyed it, the whole thing,' she says. 'I'm going to see where I can go from here.'

Jessica sits quietly sobbing. She has yet to face the judges. Michelle tells her to pull herself together. 'Do *not* do this. You've got to walk in there and be confident,' she says firmly.

Jessica wipes away her tears. 'I know that, man,' she says, mimicking Michelle's Geordie accent and attempting a smile.

Kym is called. Despite her predictions, she is through to the last day. Her Mum rings. 'Are you crying *again*?' Kym says.

Kevin is through. Jessica, too, despite her fears (and her tears) makes it. Michelle is now weeping quietly in a corner.

'I'm upset because I rang my Dad and he was crying,' she says. 'I've never heard him cry before, so that was very emotional. And they seem to be getting rid of a lot of people.'

Danny is in. Taz is out. 'I didn't get it guys,' he says. No one can believe it. 'Whoever makes it into the band, don't forget about Taz,' he says. 'I want a backstage pass to everything you do.'

Paul appears. He is also out. He remains buoyant. 'I didn't make it but I'm a star anyway,' he declares. 'Everyone here has so much talent. You're a great bunch of people – well done.'

Tears run down Kym's face. 'It never crossed my mind that these people would be going because they're all so talented,' she says. 'It's horrible, and it's hard to feel happy for yourself when everyone's so upset. There are a lot of people in tears now, crying for their friends more than anything, and it is heartbreaking.'

Myleene appears. She has made it. Again, she appears to take it in her stride. There are no tears – just the prospect of washing another top in the washbasin of her hotel bathroom that night. Raymond is the last to walk the Green Mile. He returns sobbing. Tears now run down Danny's face. For once his trademark smile has deserted him.

Eight of the group are out. The whole room is in tears as Nigel Lythgoe appears to thank them all. As he hugs each one in turn he is uncharacteristically lost for words. There are tears in his eyes. He puts his hand over the lens of a camera. 'Not for this,' he says, walking away.

Nicki Chapman appears, her face wet from crying. It was first Jessica, and then Raymond, who made her break down.

'With Raymond we could see he was absolutely shattered and you do think, my God, has he lost what he had because of us? I really hope not,' she says. 'It's never easy telling people, but Warren, Taz and Raymond were the hardest. The girls seemed to take it better. It's not that they're any less ambitious, they just seem to take it more constructively.'

Nicki has been part of plenty of auditions and seen people come and go. Nothing has ever moved her as much as *Popstars*. 'I've never encountered anything like this,' she says. 'If you'd asked me a month ago would I be getting emotional and crying *in front of them* I'd have said no. I'm amazed at how personally I'm taking it.'

She leaves vowing to wear waterproof mascara the following day.

Twenty-four hours later the judges do it all again. They pick their final ten – Kevin, Danny, Noel, Tony, Kelli, Kym, Jessica, Michelle, Myleene and Suzanne. Over the course of the next week, Nigel Lythgoe, Nicki Chapman and Paul Adam will have to choose the five who will become the band. For David, Gary, Ian and TJ the dream is over.

For the ten who have made it a tense week follows. Each one is now under contract to London Weekend Television. A week from now five will tear up those contracts. They will become the 'B' Band, for whom success may or may not follow. The remaining five will prepare for a new life.

For everyone, it has been quite a week.

Two days later an email arrives from Nigel Lythgoe. It neatly sums up the mood of what has been both an uplifting and a draining week.

He writes, 'It has never ceased to amaze me that a battle-hardened, dispassionate, old and cynical television executive could have been so affected by a bunch of hopeful and in the main naïve kids...'

Then there were Five

popstars

With the Brixton auditions over, the judges meet to decide who will be in the band. There are heated discussions as Nigel Lythgoe, Paul Adam and Nicki Chapman argue for their favourite five. Each has definite views on who should make it. For a week they put their heads together, shuffling picture cards of the final ten into different combinations of five.

'It got quite personal,' Nigel admits. 'It did get to be about looks and gut feelings about people and how they would work together.'

'There were certainly some heavy conversations,' Nicki says. 'The band I wanted I actually got – the make-believe band in my mind did fit into place. In the end, we were all in agreement: there was unity in our thoughts.'

Paul Adam recalls that choosing four of the five was relatively simple. All agreed that Danny, Kym, Noel and Myleene should be in the band. A question mark hung over the fifth person. It was between Suzanne and Kelli, both of whom had a very similar sound. In looks and temperament, however, they were chalk and cheese. It was up to the judges to decide who would fit best with the others. Suzanne, finally, won the day.

'I think we just warmed to her more,' says Paul. 'They both have similar voices and a very strong look. I think Kelli is quite controlled, and Myleene is quite similar. We felt that might upset the balance of the band.'

During the workshop at Brixton Kelli had appeared moody and the judges had urged her to smile more. Nigel Lythgoe was a big fan, but feared her true potential never came through. 'I always thought Kelli was a star,' he says. 'My colleagues thought she was just too quiet for the band.'

Inevitably, not everyone will agree with the judges, not least the five runners-up.

'There's something cynical inside me that says the British public love the underdog,' says Nigel. 'There's bound to be a lot of people saying Kevin should have been in the band or Kelli, or Tony or whoever. We had to make our decision based on what we thought would work best.'

Having agreed on the five, the judges set off separately around the country to break the news.

Suzanne was at her Nan's house in Bury, Lancashire, when Nigel arrived, camera crew in tow, to tell her she was in.

'It was a horrible day,' she recalls. 'Nigel put me through a really hard time. He told me I was the only person who split the judges decision.

> 'Nothing like this ever happens to me. I never get chosen...this is like a dream come true and I'm just going to give it my best shot.'
>
> KYM

44

When he said that I thought – I've definitely not got it!'

Having prepared herself for the worst, Suzanne was amazed when Nigel handed over a set of keys – the keys to the band's 'safe' house. She stared at them in disbelief before whooping with delight. 'I was screaming my head off – it was brilliant,' she says.

Kym was waiting for the news at home with her family in Wigan. When Paul Adam arrived he was grim-faced.

'I like Paul and we get on well,' she says, 'but that day he wouldn't even look me in the eye. It was awful and he came out with all this stuff, how they'd had to get rid of five people...I was convinced I'd not got it.'

Finally, he put her out of her misery, telling her to pack ready to move to London the following week.

'I just kept saying *ohmygod, ohmygod* – you're *joking*!' says Kym. 'I told him he was horrible for putting me through all that.'

Predictably, her Mum – who cried every day of the Brixton auditions – promptly burst into tears.

'My Mum and Dad believe in me totally and they're so proud of me,' Kym says, 'but I don't think they believed in their heart of hearts that I'd go all the way. It was such a big thing – nothing like this ever happens to me. I *never* get chosen, I was always the last one picked for sport at school, you know what I mean? This is like a dream come true and I keep thinking I'm going to wake up. I'm just going to give it my best shot.'

In Cardiff, Noel was pacing the floor. He had been primed to expect a visit from Nigel Lythgoe. On the day, however, Nigel – marooned in southern Ireland by bad weather – cancelled. Instead, Noel was told to expect Paul Adam at noon the following day. Paul finally showed eight hours late. By then, Noel was practically at breaking point.

'You can imagine how I was feeling,' he says. He was not in the mood to wait a second longer to hear whether he was in the band. 'I said, Paul, just tell me – *now!*'

If Paul had rehearsed his speech he soon abandoned it. 'He just said, "You're in!" ' says Noel, grinning at the memory. 'I said, very cool, "Oh thanks – well, I've got another meeting now..." No, just kidding! It was mad. I think my Mum was more surprised than me. '

Noel's Mum had managed to secretly blow up 67 balloons in the Welsh colours and hide them in the spare room upstairs. (Noel was number 67 at his first audition in Cardiff.) Suddenly, they all came tumbling down the stairs.

'She had all these Welsh banners and stuff,' he says. 'It was really funny, mad.'

Sworn to secrecy, Noel spent the following week preparing to leave for London.

'It did get to be about looks and gut feelings about people and how they would work together.'
NIGEL

'It was bizarre. I was saying to all my friends, I have to go away for a while. I just can't tell you where...'

Danny was at home in London with his Nan, his Mum and his aunt when he heard the news. It was Nicki who told him.

She had met Danny before *Popstars* when he auditioned for another TV show.

'Seeing Danny and saying yes to him was the highlight of my day,' she says. 'That smile, that face, that charisma, and what a voice. You can't forget the voice. I find Danny a very exciting member of the band in that respect.'

For Nigel Lythgoe, Danny's voice and his temperament sold him. 'You can judge a voice quickly but that's not all you're taking into account,' he says. 'It's this thing of putting five people together, knowing they're going to be living together; you want them to get on well.'

Danny impressed the judges throughout with his easy-going manner.

'The wonderful thing about Danny is that he is so modest, and I hope that remains,' says Nicki Chapman. 'He brings a freshness to the band and a naivety. Also, his feet are firmly on the ground – welded to the ground.'

While he was waiting for Nicki to arrive, Danny – in typical fashion – had remained laid-back. Whatever the outcome, he was happy.

'I just wanted it to be over,' Danny says, smiling. 'I was so proud of myself for just getting to the last ten. That was an achievement for me – a "No" would still have been excellent, as far as I was concerned. I wasn't really worried. I was well pleased.'

When Nicki broke the news Danny was speechless. 'In the end I just said thank you very much and gave her a kiss, then I crept into the kitchen where my family was,' he says. 'There was an eerie silence, then they gave me champagne.'

Nicki also broke the news to Myleene. She caught up with her at the Royal Academy of Music, in London.

'Because we were filming I had to walk into the building over and over again for the camera,' she says. 'I could see Myleene waiting inside and I couldn't look her in the eye – and I was telling her yes!'

Myleene believes the judges chose exactly the right characters for the band. 'There are no egos, and I think that's a lot to do with the judges,' she says. 'I can't think of anyone I'd rather be in a band with than these people, and I really mean that. For anyone looking in from the outside and waiting for the gossip – there is none! There is no "I" – we are a five.'

For the five who made it there was a week to pack and say their goodbyes. Such was the secrecy surrounding *Popstars* that even the address of their new home in

'*It was bizarre. I was saying to all my friends,
I have to go away for a while.
I just can't tell you where...*'
NOEL

'I can't think of anyone I'd rather be in a band with than these people, and I really mean that.'
MYLEENE

London was kept under wraps. For four months they would live at a secret location, their whereabouts known only to a handful of people.

Meanwhile the judges also had bad news for the five who had failed to make it. There was disappointment for Jessica, Kelli, Tony, Michelle and Kevin.

'I have done a lot of auditions over the years and had to say no to a lot of people, but I've never done it so personally, and never in front of a TV camera,' Nicki says.

'I would say this is the worst thing, professionally, I have ever had to do – and I've had to do some pretty grotty things in my life. If it was bad for me, it was a hundred times worse for them.'

'I was so proud of myself for just getting to the last ten. That was an achievement for me – a "No" would still have been excellent, as far as I was concerned.'
DANNY

'Kevin made a really valid point. He had been given a contract, seen what was on offer, and *signed* it. Then I came along and snatched it away from him, which was pretty tough.'

It was Nigel who broke the news to Michelle at her home in Newcastle.

Having come so close to a place in Girl Thing, the disappointment of seeing *Popstars* slip through her fingers was almost too much to bear.

'She was the one that broke down really badly,' Nigel recalls. 'She said she hadn't the energy to carry on in the business.' By the following day, Michelle had rallied. She was not about to throw years of training and hard work down the drain. 'She bounced straight back,' says Nigel, impressed.

He admits the audition process – and, ultimately, the rejections – proved more harrowing than he had anticipated.

'It was a very emotional process,' he says. 'They all put their talent on the line. It is tough but that's the nature of this business – you go along, show your talent, and it's bought or rejected. If you can't go through that rejection then you shouldn't come into the business.'

In Noel, Kym, Danny, Myleene and Suzanne , the judges believe they have assembled the best band from the thousands who auditioned.

'All five bring something different and they all make each other shine,' says Nicki Chapman. 'It's difficult to pinpoint just why that is but I really hope the viewers will see it. In the end, they will make up their own minds.'

Popstars at Home

In the week spent packing before their move to London all five members of the band begin speculating on their new home. None have a clue what to expect, and the production team is giving nothing away. Such is the sensitivity now surrounding *Popstars* that the location of the 'safe' house remains a closely guarded secret right up until the day they move. For the next three months, even the band's families will be unaware of its precise location.

Somehow, series producer Conrad Green has to make sure the identity of the band stays under wraps until it is revealed in the TV series on 3 February. Already, some tabloid journalists know too much, creating mild paranoia within the production team. While confidentiality agreements legally bind all those in contact with the band, Green remains nervous of leaks.

'Too many people know who they are and where they are already,' says. 'Keeping it secret is going to be tough.'

On the day they move in Danny, who has the shortest distance to travel, arrives first. Nothing has prepared him for what he finds. Home is an imposing, detached property worth a cool £1.5 million in an exclusive north London suburb.

'I was amazed. It's not what I'm used to at all,' he says later. 'They don't have houses like this in Hackney. It's like being in the countryside.'

The house, secluded and spacious, is big enough to accommodate the band and members of the production team on call 24 hours a day.

'I never imagined this fabulous house,' Kym says. 'It is beyond my wildest dreams.'

Downstairs, is a drawing room and lounge with squashy sofas, televisions, videos, DVD players, computer games and music systems. There is a conservatory (largely unused as it it the coldest room in the house) and a music and dance studio, complete with piano and mirrored wall.

In the hallway, just inside the front door, is a plaque which reads, *'Coming together is a beginning. Keeping together is progress. Working together is success.'* Upstairs, at one end of the landing, is a bedroom with en suite bathroom for use by the production team. At the other end are the band's quarters – three more bedrooms and two bathrooms. Noel and Danny share one of the rooms. Kym and Myleene are in the second shared room. Suzanne has a room to herself.

'Kym didn't want to be on her own, so we decided to share,' Myleene says. 'It has worked out really well. For me it feels like having a big sister.'

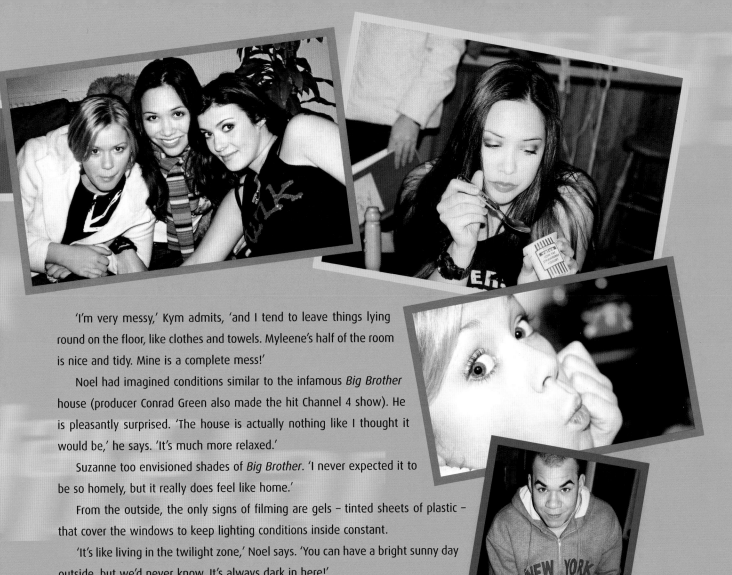

'I'm very messy,' Kym admits, 'and I tend to leave things lying round on the floor, like clothes and towels. Myleene's half of the room is nice and tidy. Mine is a complete mess!'

Noel had imagined conditions similar to the infamous *Big Brother* house (producer Conrad Green also made the hit Channel 4 show). He is pleasantly surprised. 'The house is actually nothing like I thought it would be,' he says. 'It's much more relaxed.'

Suzanne too envisioned shades of *Big Brother*. 'I never expected it to be so homely, but it really does feel like home.'

From the outside, the only signs of filming are gels – tinted sheets of plastic – that cover the windows to keep lighting conditions inside constant.

'It's like living in the twilight zone,' Noel says. 'You can have a bright sunny day outside, but we'd never know. It's always dark in here!'

After just a few hours in the house and barely unpacked, they start work. Their first meeting is with Paul Adam from Polydor and the producers from Stargate – the Norwegian recording studio behind some of S Club 7's hits. The serious business of finding their first hit single has already begun. A process that would normally take six months is about to be squeezed into eight weeks, to meet the schedule for the series.

In the coming weeks they will begin to discover the reality of life as fledgling pop stars. They will work long, unpredictable hours. They will miss meals and abandon everyday activities like shopping and cooking. Their consumption of takeaways and junk food – for convenience sake – will soar. They will grow used to living in a cocoon with cameras recording every aspect of their lives.

A few miles away, in his office high above London's South Bank, Nigel Lythgoe reflects on what has been a gruelling few months. From the thousands who auditioned, he has his band. Now the pressure is on to create a top-rated TV show and turn five talented unknowns into stars. There are not enough hours in the day. *Popstars* is spilling over into evenings and weekends.

49

DID YOU KNOW?

Danny started singing just three years ago. He got up in a karaoke bar in Tenerife on holiday and never looked back! Before his big break with Popstars he was working part-time as a cleaner.

He is his usual well-pressed self but, unusually, is unshaven. He rubs his chin. 'Can't find my razor,' he says. 'Everything's a bit all over the place just now.'

More than anyone, perhaps, he understands that adjusting to stardom will inevitably take its toll on the five. His instinct is to protect them.

'Their lives have changed just like that,' he says. 'The most difficult thing is going to be that the public think they own them. A few weeks from now they will be recognised wherever they go – they have yet to experience that.'

The theme from *Mission Impossible* strikes up on his mobile phone. 'That's the band,' he says, rummaging in his pockets and finding the missing razor. Myleene is calling from Sheffield, where they are midway through their first recording session. All is well. The band have agreed on a name – *HEAR'SAY*. Nigel has invited suggestions from the *Popstars* team and offered a magnum of champagne for the best. Ideas are pouring in.

'Look, for all five of you to agree on something so quickly is terrific,' he tells her. He rolls his eyes. 'No, Myleene, you *don't* get to win the champagne. You're *giving* it...'

Elsewhere, the *Popstars* machine gathers momentum. Charlie Donaldson, Granada Media's Head of Licensing, is working on ideas for merchandise. The series – regarded by many as the new *Big Brother* – is generating massive interest. The clamour to know the identity of the band grows louder every day, yet even Donaldson does not know who the five are.

'It is difficult trying to sell something when you can't tell people what they're buying,' he says, 'but in a way the secrecy makes it more exciting. It creates a buzz.'

Discussions, meanwhile, are underway for a package of merchandise, ranging from *Popstars* pyjamas to tee shirts, cosmetics and CD-ROMs, a board game – and dolls.

Production on prototypes has already begun. By Easter 2001 the dolls will be in the shops. 'Normally, we would have six months in development but in this case there is just six weeks,'

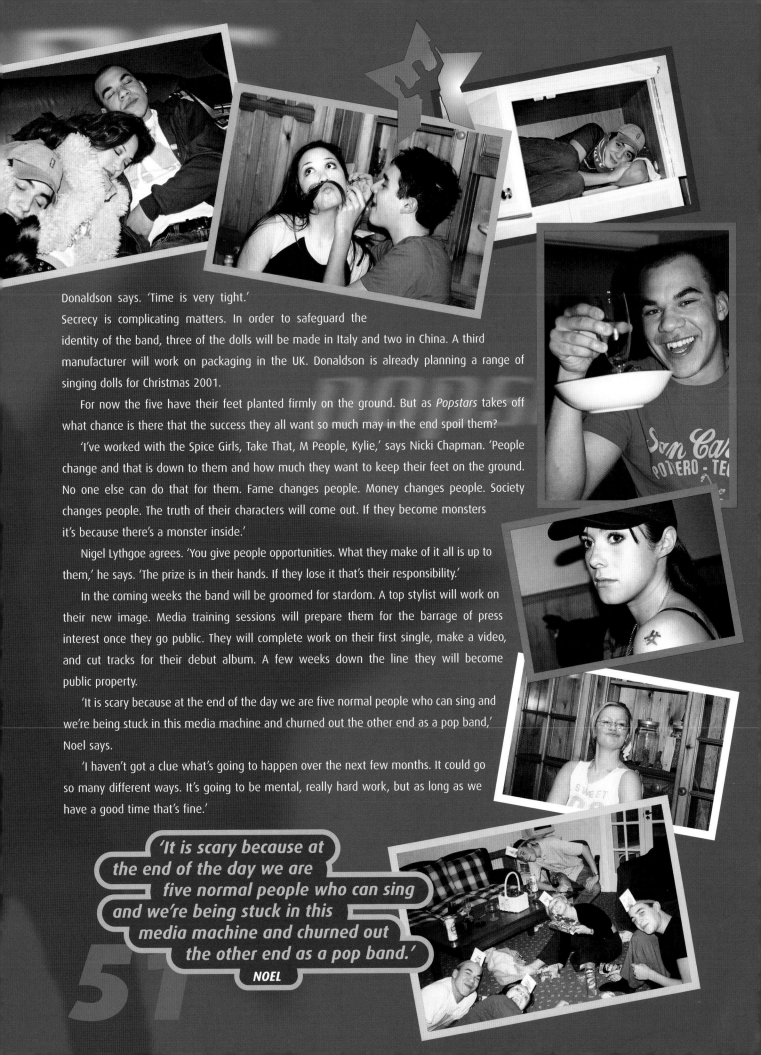

Donaldson says. 'Time is very tight.'

Secrecy is complicating matters. In order to safeguard the identity of the band, three of the dolls will be made in Italy and two in China. A third manufacturer will work on packaging in the UK. Donaldson is already planning a range of singing dolls for Christmas 2001.

For now the five have their feet planted firmly on the ground. But as *Popstars* takes off what chance is there that the success they all want so much may in the end spoil them?

'I've worked with the Spice Girls, Take That, M People, Kylie,' says Nicki Chapman. 'People change and that is down to them and how much they want to keep their feet on the ground. No one else can do that for them. Fame changes people. Money changes people. Society changes people. The truth of their characters will come out. If they become monsters it's because there's a monster inside.'

Nigel Lythgoe agrees. 'You give people opportunities. What they make of it all is up to them,' he says. 'The prize is in their hands. If they lose it that's their responsibility.'

In the coming weeks the band will be groomed for stardom. A top stylist will work on their new image. Media training sessions will prepare them for the barrage of press interest once they go public. They will complete work on their first single, make a video, and cut tracks for their debut album. A few weeks down the line they will become public property.

'It is scary because at the end of the day we are five normal people who can sing and we're being stuck in this media machine and churned out the other end as a pop band,' Noel says.

'I haven't got a clue what's going to happen over the next few months. It could go so many different ways. It's going to be mental, really hard work, but as long as we have a good time that's fine.'

'It is scary because at the end of the day we are five normal people who can sing and we're being stuck in this media machine and churned out the other end as a pop band.'

NOEL

51

Kym

Name:	**Kimberley Marsh**
DOB:	**13/6/76**
Star Sign:	**Gemini**

Kym almost didn't make it to the *Popstars* auditions and never expected to make it into the band. In the space of a few weeks her life has changed beyond recognition.

'I don't think it has sunk in properly yet,' she says. 'Suddenly, we're having to be secretive about everything. We can't go out as a five. We can't even go to the supermarket together.'

The secrecy will end only when their identity is revealed midway through the *Popstars* series. 'It does get a bit scary,' says Kym, 'because it's not going to get any better. Once it's out in the open it's actually going to get worse.'

Kym is steeling herself for the moment she will be thrust into the public eye. 'If people look at us and think we've made it overnight then they don't know our backgrounds,' she says. 'Each and every one of us has a story to tell and mine has been a struggle.'

At school such was her dedication to singing and dancing that she was bullied. 'I was always doing a show or something so I never hung round the discos, never had a boyfriend. I was always being called a square. And because I didn't have a boyfriend I had to be gay, you know, which I'm not.'

Kym reckons being bullied toughened her up. 'It didn't do me any harm in the end,' she says. 'In fact I grew and became a much stronger person because of it.'

In some respects Kym is glad she had to wait until the age of 24 for her big break. 'I think I'm wiser now,' she says. 'I've had knock backs and I could have just laid down and not got back up, but I did.'

Through thick and thin it was her parents who supported her. Kym is incredibly close to them – and hugely proud of her northern roots.

'I think a lot of people forget where they came from – they might have lived on a council estate or been on the dole, or whatever,' she says. 'I never want to forget and I don't honestly think my parents would let me. That's a steadying influence. I will never forget where I'm from or what I've done in the past.'

As a child, much of Kym's inspiration came from her Dad, whose own band – Ricky and The Dominant Four – played gigs at Liverpool's legendary Cavern Club, sometimes supporting The Beatles. What makes Kym's success particularly poignant is that six years ago her Dad was dangerously ill after suffering a heart attack. It was the most devastating experience of her life. When Kym dashed to the hospital she found her Mum sobbing in the corridor and her Dad in a critical condition.

'They say the first 24 hours are crucial,' she says. 'I'm not deeply religious but I do believe in God, and that night I prayed, please, please.'

Her prayers were answered. Today, Kym's Dad is fit and well. 'He's so full of life now you'd never guess what he went through. He's lovely – both my parents are. They would do anything for me – as I would for them.'

Having won a place in the hottest new band of 2001 she is determined to keep her feet firmly on the ground. 'The world around me is going to change but I don't want to change,' she says. 'I'm a normal person, except I've been given this great chance by people who have decided I'm talented enough and I'm grateful – it could quite easily have been someone else. It doesn't make me the best just because I'm here.'

Kym knows that rarely do pop stars remain down to earth. She and Myleene had a reminder of what fame can bring when they went to see one of their favourite bands, Five, performing at Wembley Stadium in December. The girls went incognito to the after-show party hoping to meet the band.

'No one knew what we were doing there. People were looking at us as if, who are they?' says Kym. When they sat on a sofa reserved for Five they were quickly shooed away by minders. 'I really want us to be normal,' she says. 'At this stage, before anyone knows who we are, it's easy to observe and see what you don't want to be like.'

Sharing the house has meant all five band members have had to form relationships fast.

'Everyone gets on so well and that's the most important thing. We've got this thing about solidarity,' Kym says.

She has decided to have a third – and final – tattoo dedicated to the others. 'It will be my symbol to them to show my loyalty,' she says. 'It's like an engagement between myself and the others. I want to look back in years to come on this period of my life and remember what I was doing and what it meant to me.'

53

Suzanne

Name: **Suzanne Shaw**
DOB: **29/9/81**
Star Sign: **Libra**

Suzanne is the baby of the band. She sits curled up on a sofa with her jeans rolled up to her knees to reveal an angry red rash. 'I don't know what it is – I think maybe I'm allergic to the soap powder we're using,' she says.

Suzanne is still adjusting to being in the band. 'It's like, this is crazy,' she says. That morning she had seen a trailer running on ITV for *Popstars*.

'It was a total reality check for me,' she says. 'I thought – that's all about us. I'm part of the band. It really is mad and I don't think it has sunk in yet.'

Like Kym, Suzanne, recognises the importance of remaining down to earth. 'I'm really no different to anyone else out there,' she says. 'I've just decided to go into this business because it's what I enjoy.'

She accepts that change is inevitable. 'I've changed already,' she says. 'Some of it will probably go to my head, but I'm just hoping if I ever get too big for my boots someone will give me a slap. Never do I want to say the words, "Do you know who I am!" '

'Some of it will probably go to my head, but I'm just hoping if I ever get too big for my boots someone will give me a slap.'

Suzanne has quickly become accustomed to having a camera present round the clock. Viewers will see the band at their best – and sometimes at their worst. During the auditions at Brixton, Suzanne loved having cameras around, saying they made her feel 'a million dollars.' Since moving into the house, however, she admits there have been moments when she has longed for them to stop rolling.

'Sometimes you're tired and suddenly the camera's on you and you're being asked questions,' she says. 'You do think, enough's enough. There have been times when we've all said, *please*.'

She wonders what the viewers will make of it all.

'I sometimes think am I going to look like a fool?' she says. 'How are the public going to perceive us, especially me? It's the whole *Big Brother* thing. You wonder if people will be saying, oh we love Noel – he's dead funny – but Suzy's a bit mousey, you know?'

Suzanne's boyfriend, Andrew, is a steadying influence when panic threatens to set in. The pair sang together in The Right Stuff before Suzanne got her Popstars break. They have been dating 18 months.

'We're not dead serious but we're there for each other,' she says. 'It's good to have someone to share things with and he totally understands. I'm so lucky to have that. I used to be insecure and neurotic and he has taught me not to get stressed out about the little things.'

Since moving into the house Suzanne has not seen much of Andrew, but they talk constantly on the phone. She admits her mobile phone might as well be grafted onto the side of her head! Her last monthly bill was a whopping £200!

'I know I'm always on the phone and the others tease me about it,' she says, 'but I need to keep in touch. It's my lifeline. And, anyway, Myleene is much worse than me!'

Danny

Name: Danny Foster
DOB: 3/5/79
Star Sign: Taurus

'I never thought I'd be here,' Danny says. 'I don't think it was so much low confidence, more that I'm a quiet person, not in your face. I knew I wanted to be in a band, but I didn't think I'd be picked for a TV series.'

Like the others, Danny has pledged not to let fame rush to his head. He wants to keep both feet firmly on the ground, whatever happens around him. He believes he can safeguard elements of his old life, however much he is in the spotlight.

'I'm not really worried about the fame thing,' he says. 'It will be interesting to do good music and be successful for that. I'd rather be known for my music than anything else.'

During his first few weeks in the house he has managed to slip back home to East London to spend time with his family and friends. Leaving the cocoon of the *Popstars* house, even briefly, has been good for him.

'We're not exactly in a bubble but we're in a strange environment and there's a lot we can't do – like go out together. It's good to step away from that now and then.'

On one trip home Danny rode the Tube wondering how much longer he would be able to move around London unnoticed on public transport.

'It's weird,' he says. 'But I think it is possible to stay true to yourself. At one stage at the auditions I wondered if I should be jumping in front of the cameras to get noticed. But what's the point of that? It's such an immense pressure if you're going to put on an act.' He grins. 'And even though I didn't say much I still got here, which is cool, and I'm proud of that.'

Danny's life is already starting to change. One major breakthrough is that he has learned to use an iron! 'I never normally wear shirts but I got one the night we went to *An Audience With Ricky Martin*,' he says. 'It was brand new in a packet and all creased. I had to ring my

56

Nan to find out how to iron it. It took me 40 minutes and it was still all creased!'

Housework is not a problem, however. Danny's old job as an office cleaner stands him in good stead. 'I'm not afraid of that. We all just do our bit. There's no rota or anything.'

He cannot cook, though. 'It's not my strong point. If I did it they'd all go down with food poisoning,' he says. Noel's brilliant. He did this amazing pasta dish the other night. I thought it was from M & S – that's how good it was!'

Danny was thinking about training as a teacher when he discovered he could sing. The teaching went on the back burner while he started going to auditions. 'I knew I wanted to teach from an early age,' he says, 'and I know it's always something I can go back to.'

Like Suzanne, he is in a serious relationship. He has been with his girlfriend Chloe, a media studies student, for three years. The pair speak daily on the phone but with Danny in the band, and Chloe at university, their time together is precious.

'Everything is really cool,' he says. 'I'm just Danny to her. She's not fazed by any of this. We've every intention of staying together and I think we will.'

Kym bursts into the room, her hair covered in dye, her hands encased in a pair of protective gloves. 'I'm doing my roots,' she announces. Noel follows, recording the interruption on a neat little video camera. Myleene arrives with a stills camera.

'Excuse me,' Noel says, bearing down on Danny with the video camera. 'Just how interesting has all this been?'

Danny grins. Kym waves a gloved hand. 'Where's the camera? We need a still of me doing my roots.'

Myleene crouches at the end of the sofa with her camera. 'This is a good shot. 'I'm getting a picture of Noel getting a picture of me – a photo within a photo!'

Danny grins. 'Sorry about the interruption,' Myleene says as the three retreat. 'What can I tell you about the other band members?' says Danny. He raises his voice. 'Well, Noel's a right idiot...' The door flies open and Noel is back. 'I want to hear this,' he says. Danny rolls his eyes. 'He talks in his sleep. All the time. Every night. He shouts.'

Noel grins. 'My Mum says I only do that when I'm stressed. What could I possibly be stressed about...?'

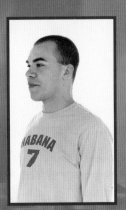

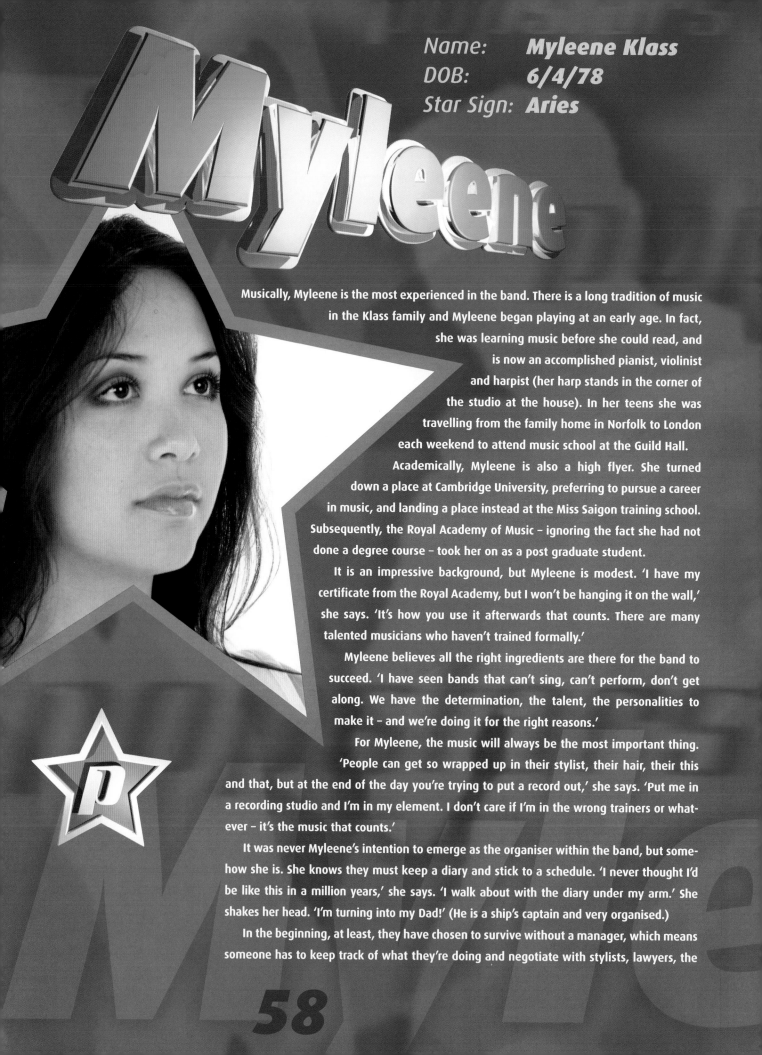

Myleene

Musically, Myleene is the most experienced in the band. There is a long tradition of music in the Klass family and Myleene began playing at an early age. In fact, she was learning music before she could read, and is now an accomplished pianist, violinist and harpist (her harp stands in the corner of the studio at the house). In her teens she was travelling from the family home in Norfolk to London each weekend to attend music school at the Guild Hall.

Academically, Myleene is also a high flyer. She turned down a place at Cambridge University, preferring to pursue a career in music, and landing a place instead at the Miss Saigon training school. Subsequently, the Royal Academy of Music – ignoring the fact she had not done a degree course – took her on as a post graduate student.

It is an impressive background, but Myleene is modest. 'I have my certificate from the Royal Academy, but I won't be hanging it on the wall,' she says. 'It's how you use it afterwards that counts. There are many talented musicians who haven't trained formally.'

Myleene believes all the right ingredients are there for the band to succeed. 'I have seen bands that can't sing, can't perform, don't get along. We have the determination, the talent, the personalities to make it – and we're doing it for the right reasons.'

For Myleene, the music will always be the most important thing. 'People can get so wrapped up in their stylist, their hair, their this and that, but at the end of the day you're trying to put a record out,' she says. 'Put me in a recording studio and I'm in my element. I don't care if I'm in the wrong trainers or whatever – it's the music that counts.'

It was never Myleene's intention to emerge as the organiser within the band, but somehow she is. She knows they must keep a diary and stick to a schedule. 'I never thought I'd be like this in a million years,' she says. 'I walk about with the diary under my arm.' She shakes her head. 'I'm turning into my Dad!' (He is a ship's captain and very organised.)

In the beginning, at least, they have chosen to survive without a manager, which means someone has to keep track of what they're doing and negotiate with stylists, lawyers, the

record company, the *Popstars* production team, and others. That someone is usually Myleene. 'We've had to do things for ourselves and look at the bigger picture instead of just being chauffeured round, waiting for things to happen.'

All five have clear ideas about image, music, deals – and the direction they want to take. 'I'm not easily intimidated by meetings,' Myleene says. 'And a lot of our strength comes from our unity. I know we have the upper hand because we work as a five, we speak as a five, and people treat us as a five.'

Myleene loves the atmosphere in the house. 'It's a big house and we could all go off and have our space but we don't. We all crowd into the same room – you've seen that!'

On cue, Noel appears. 'Is this the *Magna Carta* you're doing or what? He says.

'It's *War and Peace*,' Myleene tells him.

'I think I've got SAD (Seasonal Affective Disorder),' he says. 'I don't want to do anything today (it is 3p.m. and he still hasn't showered...)

'What's wrong with me? I'm sitting in a one-and-a-half-million-pound house listening to our tracks, done by top producers, waiting to be interviewed for our book, and I just want to sleep...!' He bursts out laughing.

'Reality check!' says Myleene. 'It is strange because we're living in a bubble here – not a bad bubble, but it's so weird when you leave it. Danny and I have both been home and it's so strange...'

Noel interrupts. 'Danny doesn't think it's as strange as you do...'

'You wait 'til you get back to Cardiff for Christmas – you'll see.' She grins. 'I can't wait to get home and just veg out. You know how people get all dressed up to eat their Christmas dinner? We all wear our pyjamas!'

Noel says, 'I'll be in my new Christmas pants and socks.'

'I'll have new slippers and a dressing gown-'

'And my new jumper,' says Noel. 'That's before I try out my new bubble bath.'

'I always get magnolia bubble bath,' Myleene says.

Noel frowns. 'Magnolia? Are you sure you're not mixing up your present with someone else's? Er, some older person...'

'My Dad makes me write to Santa or I don't get a present.'

Noel stares at her. 'That's strange, Myleene. That is so freaky. I'm not speaking to you any more...' He backs out of the room. 'And get a move on!'

Myleene smiles. 'I told you no one's allowed in a room by themselves – not for more than a few minutes anyway!' she says.

Noel

Name: *Noel Sullivan*
DOB: *28/7/80*
Star Sign: *Leo*

Ask anyone about Noel and they'll tell you he is a brilliant mimic, always doing impressions. He is also refreshingly down to earth. And, when the wisecracks stop, there is a serious side to him. For years he has wanted to be a performer. Now that he has made it into the *Popstars* band he is on Cloud Nine. What he is not so sure about is the inevitable overnight exposure that he and the others will face.

'I'm really scared about the whole thing,' he admits. 'Basically, I want to sing and dance and that's about it. I'm not bothered about having my face in the papers. I suppose that's all part and parcel of it – you can't have one without the other.'

Just days after the band moved in together they had a taste of what was to come when Nigel Lythgoe arranged for them to go to the recording of *An Audience with Ricky Martin* at the LWT studios. 'We were meant to be incognito and we weren't at all,' he recalls. 'We pulled up at the studios in a car together and all the paparazzi were there, so we were all photographed. We were escorted through the queue to our seats, right at the front, and you could just see people thinking, Who are they?'

At the party after the show the five – posing as competition winners – mingled with celebrity guests. They were snapped with Emma Bunton and her cousin. 'I kept thinking that soon people are going to know who I am, what I look like when I get up in the morning, what I'm like when I lose my rag – all that kind of stuff,' he says.

'The most bizarre thing is they're talking about doing *An Audience* with us, so all those celebrities will be there to watch us!' He bursts out laughing. 'It's mad!'

Since moving in with the others Noel has not only emerged as the joker – he has also proved himself a terrific cook. Sadly, none of his culinary exploits have been captured on camera (yet).

'They've missed it every time,' he says, laughing. ' They started to film me the other night and I just said, "Go away!" It was 11p.m. and I knew it was going to take me a couple of hours to cook and I just didn't want the whole thing on camera.'

At times, everyone has grown weary of the constant presence of the cameras. There has been the occasional mutiny when directors Danny Fildes and David O'Neill have met with resistance from all five. 'Sometimes we give them some grief, but that's to be expected.'

They are all anxious that what ends up on camera is as spontaneous as it can be. 'You do something off the cuff which might be funny or interesting and the crew suddenly want to film it. They'll say, "Can you just do that again please?" ' Noel says. 'That ruins it, 'cause we're not actors. It's meant to be fly on the wall, not *Hamlet*, so we say "NO!" '

Mainly, the relationship between the band and the production team is good. Again, it is based on respect. Danny Fildes, David O'Neill, Luke Dolan and Louise Cowmeadow, who take it in turns to stay at the house, are mates.

Noel is surprised at how well the five band members get along.

'There's a mutual respect there, because we all know what we've been through to get here – and what we've been through personally as well.'

All have struggled for their big break. Noel has spent five years trying to break into the music industry. For a year before *Popstars* came along he was working in Ibiza in a cabaret show. 'I was on stage dressed in black working under ultra violet light with something like 150 puppets. It was a really clever show.' After a year, it was time to move on. 'I just woke up one morning and decided to come home and go for every audition I could,' he says.

Personally, Noel has faced more than his share of tragedy. When he was six, his baby brother was a cot death victim. Three years later his baby sister died from a brain tumour at just nine days old. It all served to cement the close relationship he has with his Mum.

'That's why I'm doing this really,' he says. It's not for selfish reasons. I want to be able to look after her.'

Another factor is his eight-year-old cousin, Luke, who is suffering from cancer of the muscle and battling with bouts of serious illness. The pair are very close. 'I know how much it will mean for Luke to see me on TV. It's a huge thing for him, and that makes whatever else you have to go through on the way worthwhile.'

The Band on The Band

'If you could roll them into one they would be the perfect person.'
SUZANNE

KYM SAYS... 'Noel is very funny – he's going to make you laugh. He sleepwalks and talks in his sleep. Very loudly. Poor Danny gets woken up every night. Myleene is terrible for getting up in the morning. She loves her bed. Danny has no bad habits(!). He is the strong, silent type, but he's murder for cleaning up. He's always tidying. Suzanne is so funny – she's always getting her words mixed up. And she is always on the phone. Her brain's going to be shrivelled. I've got incredibly smelly feet! I used to wear trainers without socks and they stank. The others wouldn't even pick my trainers up off the floor, they were that bad... now I wear socks – it's band orders! I have more make-up than anyone else, but I don't use it all. I just won't chuck it away, so when something's finished I put it back in the bag rather than the bin. I'm terrible. I've got loads – and it's all rubbish!'

NOEL SAYS... 'Kym is mad – her feet really stink! That's her trademark. We all made her buy socks. Myleene is the leader. She deals with the lawyers and the TV company and the record company. She has a good business head on her shoulders, which often performers don't, so that's great. Danny is fantastic. I thought it would be really hard to share a room with someone I don't know, but we're best mates. We've not had one cross word. He's really strong and he has the same insecurities as me about fame and all that. Suzanne – well, Suzanne is the blonde...! She's lovely. She is on the phone all the time. She'll get a tumour first!'

SUZANNE SAYS... 'Noel is the joker. He's very comical and constantly has you in stitches. He does impressions all the time. Danny was quiet at first but now he's started mucking about. Kym is very straightforward – she would stick up for all of us. She is very protective. She used to have smelly feet – my pet hate! – but she doesn't any more. Her trainers stank, but she has chucked them now and got new ones. Myleene is the organiser. She keeps us level-headed. They've all got the kind of qualities you'd like in yourself. If you could roll them into one they would be the perfect person.'

MYLEENE SAYS... 'Noel loves to do the cooking and everything has to be perfect. He was making shepherd's pie the other night and we had to wait about three hours for it. The mashed potatoes didn't just have to be mashed, they had to be creamed. You weren't allowed to stop mashing until your arm hurt! Kym is very sure, but very sensitive – people don't always see that. She is beautiful and doesn't know it. She always wants to watch a video last thing at night, then she'll pass out and I'll end up watching it on my own while she snores! Kym has a carrier bag full of make-up she never uses. The whole bag nearly went in the bin the other day. Noel was cleaning up and mistook it for rubbish! Suzanne is the baby of the group. She is permanently on the phone. Danny is very peaceful and has a big grin full-time. He's a real London boy, always saying, "Be lucky!" He's also very kind. We've got very similar taste in clothes. If I was a guy I'd dress like Danny. I'm always wearing his clothes.'

DANNY SAYS... 'Myleene is amazing. She can play, she can dance, she can sing. I call her our musical director. Suzanne is very balanced. One minute she's quiet, the next she can be very funny. Kym is straight-forward. I like that. You know where you stand. She and Noel are always playing off one another. We all just giggle all the time. Noel is the impressionist, always making you laugh. He even takes me off now – the Cockney accent! I'm the quiet one, but I'm comfortable with that.'

Popstars at Work

> 'We're going to stick together through thick and thin. In this pop star bubble it's the five of us against the world.'
>
> NOEL

It's 19 December and there's less than a week to go before Christmas. The band is in the middle of a hectic recording schedule. The pressure is on to find a song that will be a smash hit first single.

Already, they have done sessions with Elliot Kennedy in Sheffield, who has worked with the Spice Girls, Five and Celine Dion, among others. A week in his Sheffield studio produced the makings of three tracks.

They have also spent a week at Stargate in Norway. A further five-and-a-half tracks came out of that session.

As the search continues for the first single Paul Adam, of Polydor, is beginning to feel the pressure. He needs two singles ready by the end of January, and an album delivered by mid February. Vital days will be lost over Christmas and New Year.

'I've already found some good songs, but I want to know I've got two or three hit singles. I've never known such pressure,' he says.

'I'm very clear about the sound. It has to be quite mature. Imagine mixing All Saints with three, four- and five-part harmonies. Songs to show off their vocal talent and set them apart.

'I'm trying to end up with a pop album that hopefully people like me would buy, but will also appeal to eight-year-olds who buy Steps. I think we can do that.'

At Mayfair Studios in north London the band is due to start work on a track called Pure and Simple with writer/producers Tim Hawes and Pete Kirtley.

An impressive slate of artists has recorded at Mayfair over the years, including Tina Turner, Blur, OMD, Bryan Adams and Sneaker Pimps. Gold and platinum discs crowd the walls in the dimly lit reception area.

When the band arrive, piling out of a people carrier, they are too preoccupied to notice their surroundings.

That morning Charlie Donaldson, Granada's Head of Licensing, has met with them to talk about the *Popstars* dolls. Kym, Danny, Myleene, Suzanne and Noel have just come face to face with themselves in doll form.

Noel is shaking his head in disbelief. 'Mine was just like me. It even had that little bit of flesh here,' he says, tilting his head up and stroking his chin. He looks around at the others. 'Did you see my chin on that doll? My *chins*.'

Danny is mildly horrified. The dolls are just too real. 'Mine was exactly like me,' he says. 'Unbelievable.'

Kym is indignant. 'I couldn't believe how ugly mine was. She pulls a face. 'It had a big round

65

face. Like this.' She puffs her cheeks out to demonstrate. 'Am I *really* that ugly?'

There is a plan to make singing versions of the dolls for Christmas. This is news to them. They all shriek at the prospect. '*Singing*? No!' Kym says. 'This is freaky.'

A few days earlier Kym has had a third – and final – tattoo etched at the base of her spine. It is the Chinese symbol meaning 'together' and neatly sums up her feelings for the band. The others are considering whether to have one too. Noel and Myleene are the only ones who don't already have tattoos. Both admit they are squeamish about the pain.

Danny reassures them. 'It doesn't really hurt. It's more of an irritation.'

Kym says, 'It does hurt, but if it's something you want you'll put up with the pain.' (Their dolls will also have tiny replicas of their tattoos.)

For Kym, the toughest part of being a pop star is spending time away from her children - five-year-old David, and Emily, aged three.

'I knew what I was letting myself in for and I knew it would be really hard,' she says. 'I don't get to see them as much as I want and that gets me down.'

Kym knew from the outset that being in the band would mean moving to London without David and Emily. She also knew that for the first few weeks at least she would be living in a secret location and would barely see them.

'I stay in touch all the time,' she says. 'I speak to them every morning and every night. If they're in bed I get my Mum to go up and kiss them and tell them I love them. It's just nice to hear their voices saying, "I love you, Mummy." That's brilliant.'

Although it is hard to be apart from them, Kym believes it will be worthwhile in the end. Having a pop star for a Mum will give her children the kind of life they could otherwise only dream about.

'First and foremost, I am doing this for them,' she says. 'I don't want to struggle, I don't want them to "make do". I want them to have the best of everything and that's why I'm doing this.'

Her kids mean everything to her. 'They are my world. I live and breathe for them,' she says. 'I had my first baby, David, when I was 18. Before that I was just busy enjoying myself, out having a laugh, and living life for me, but once you have children you start living for them and trying to make life better for them.'

Kym knows she won't be apart from her children for long. 'It's a temporary separation and it's not as if they're with strangers. They're with their grandparents and their father, and that's the best thing for them if I'm not around. We'll be back together as soon as possible.'

Kym *At 17 Kym landed her only 'proper' job – as a hotel receptionist. 'It was at the Park Hall Hotel in Charnock Richard, Lancashire. I was their worst employee – I lasted eight months. Actually, they seemed quite shocked when I left...'*

DID YOU KNOW?

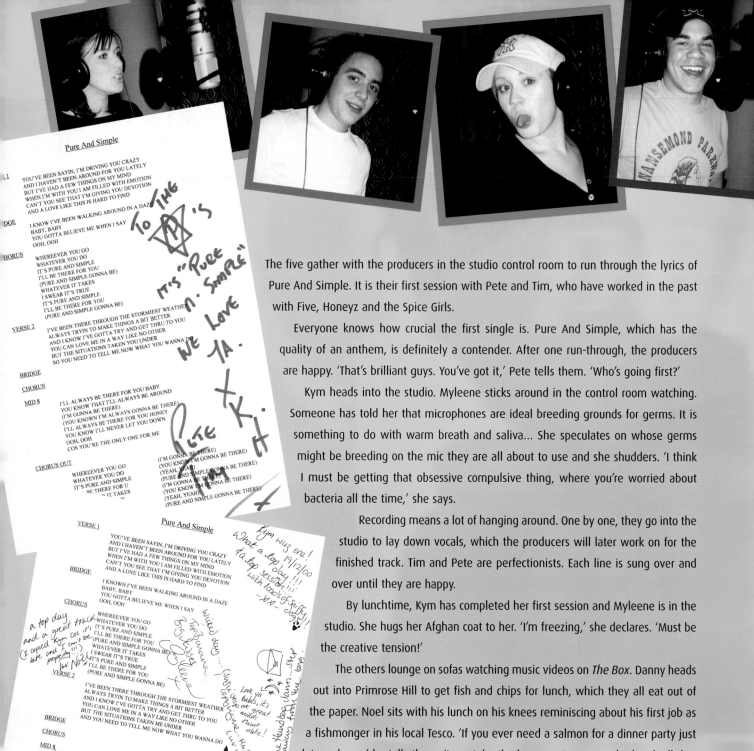

The five gather with the producers in the studio control room to run through the lyrics of Pure And Simple. It is their first session with Pete and Tim, who have worked in the past with Five, Honeyz and the Spice Girls.

Everyone knows how crucial the first single is. Pure And Simple, which has the quality of an anthem, is definitely a contender. After one run-through, the producers are happy. 'That's brilliant guys. You've got it,' Pete tells them. 'Who's going first?'

Kym heads into the studio. Myleene sticks around in the control room watching. Someone has told her that microphones are ideal breeding grounds for germs. It is something to do with warm breath and saliva... She speculates on whose germs might be breeding on the mic they are all about to use and she shudders. 'I think I must be getting that obsessive compulsive thing, where you're worried about bacteria all the time,' she says.

Recording means a lot of hanging around. One by one, they go into the studio to lay down vocals, which the producers will later work on for the finished track. Tim and Pete are perfectionists. Each line is sung over and over until they are happy.

By lunchtime, Kym has completed her first session and Myleene is in the studio. She hugs her Afghan coat to her. 'I'm freezing,' she declares. 'Must be the creative tension!'

The others lounge on sofas watching music videos on *The Box*. Danny heads out into Primrose Hill to get fish and chips for lunch, which they all eat out of the paper. Noel sits with his lunch on his knees reminiscing about his first job as a fishmonger in his local Tesco. 'If you ever need a salmon for a dinner party just let me know,' he tells them. 'I can take the bones out, remove the head, all that stuff.' He grins. 'That job was *minging* – no one would come near me. I *stank!*'

They all feel they're eating too much junk food, but working long days and odd hours is making it difficult to eat healthy meals at normal times. When they get home at night, unwind, and start to cook it can be after midnight. Their body clocks have gone slightly haywire.

Danny, who used to work out regularly before joining the band, feels the need for some serious exercise. 'I've got to get to the gym,' he says.

'I am *so* big,' says Kym. 'That's my New Year resolution – to sort out my weight.'

Noel rolls his eyes. 'Yeah, Kym – there's big and there's big...' he says.

'I know – there's bhuna big and there's Kym,' she tells him.

Suzanne has also made a resolution. Much to everyone's relief she has decided to stop using her mobile phone as much. 'It's probably too late. I've probably already got a tumour,' she says, unconcerned.

Noel stands sideways and points at his stomach. 'Look at that,' he says, jabbing at it. 'I'm not even breathing out.' He resolves to get in shape for the New Year. 'If my doll's going to have a six pack I'd better have one too,' he laughs.

'I still can't believe those dolls,' says Kym.

Myleene also has some resolutions. 'To eat less chocolate,' she says firmly. She is also a habitual user of her mobile phone. Much worse, it turns out, than Suzanne. Her last (monthly) bill was a whopping £680. 'I'm going to stop burning my brain on my phone,' she says. 'That won't happen either...' All five have new mobiles, courtesy of LWT with calls paid for by the TV company. The first bills have yet to come in.

They all pile back into the studio control room while Suzanne begins her first vocal session of the day. Despite dosing up on antihistamines, she still has a rash on her arms and legs. More worrying, she has a cold that will not shift. The previous week saw her seeking expert advice from an ear, nose and throat specialist.

Urged on by the others, she manages some difficult top notes. Pete hugs her when she finally emerges from the studio grinning. 'You star,' he says. 'You're a fighter. Well done.'

Pete and Tim, who have grabbed lunch at the control desk, decide to take a short break. 'Two minutes, guys, then we'll carry on.'

Noel slips into Pete's chair. 'Hurry up, I haven't got all day!' he tells him, surveying the mass of faders and switches in front of him.

'Captain's log, Stardate 19/12/2000...' he says, mimicking Star Trek's Captain Kirk.

67

'We have passed thousands of inferior species on our way. The crew and I are now journeying to Planet Pop!'

Once in the studio, he runs through the chorus of Pure and Simple. 'That's a nice tone you've got there, mate,' Pete tells him.

They start recording and Noel stumbles on the first line.

'Stop trying to change our lyrics!' Pete says.

Noel grins. 'If they weren't so pants I wouldn't have to!'

Danny is last up. Tim and Pete encourage him to sing an octave higher than he normally would. He is not convinced. 'It doesn't feel comfortable. Are you sure it sounds all right? It sounds *pants* to me,' he says.

Myleene, lounging on the sofa at the back of the control room, says, 'Don't hold back, Danny – tell us what you really think!'

'It's wicked, mate,' Tim tells him.

Pete agrees. 'You've got a really nice grain to your voice,' he says.

Danny wavers. 'It sounds a bit squeaky to me.'

'It just puts what's needed into the chorus – a bit of gravel,' Tim says.

Before they can get any further the fire alarm sounds. It clangs for several minutes, although there is no fire. An engineer appears but cannot turn it off. 'Funny,' Noel says. 'This happened to us at Stargate too – our vocals are just so hot!'

By mid afternoon they have all recorded their first few lines. Once the session is over, Tim and Pete will begin to 'comp' the track – taking the best lines from each one's vocals for the final version of the song. It will take another day to do the final mix. Everyone is working against the clock. With the first episode of *Popstars* due on air in just three weeks, time is at a premium.

Noel, meanwhile, sits at the piano in an empty studio nearby and works on a song of his own. By early evening he has drafted some lyrics. It is a haunting love song. 'That's so sad,' Myleene tells him. He shrugs, shoving the words into the pocket of his jeans. 'Ah well, you can only write about what you know...' he says.

Dinner is another takeaway, this time from an Italian restaurant around the corner.

They are all in high spirits. Kym finds a witch's hat and parades around in it.

Noel says his feet are starting to rot.

'I'm spending so much time in hot studios that when I take my trainers off at the

DID YOU KNOW?

The band already have nicknames – thanks to Noel. *Myleene is Mimi, Kym is Kiki, Danny is Didi, Suzanne is Sisi, and Noel is Nini. At home, Kym is known as Trio. 'There used to be an ad for a chocolate bar called Trio and the girl in the ad had the biggest mouth. That's me!' she says.*

end of the day my feet are soaking,' he says.

'You need thick socks,' Danny tells him.

'I just think I have very sweaty feet,' Noel says, frowning.

They all pile back into the studio for one final exuberant chorus. The five stand, arms draped round each others shoulders, swaying from side to side.

'Noel keeps spitting on the mic!' says Kym.

'She's lucky that's all I'm spitting at,' he says.

It's is 10.30p.m. when they finish. They will be home by 11p.m., but it will be hours before they all unwind.

The next day will see them in another studio with different producers, working on a new track. In three days they will be going home for their last Christmas as unknowns. All are determined to make the most of it. Already their lives are different, but they know that far bigger changes lie ahead. They are on the brink of fame and fortune, poised to become the biggest new band of 2001. Nothing will ever be quite the same again.

'We don't want anything to go wrong,' Noel says. 'We're going to stick together through thick and thin as a five. The protection is there. In this pop star bubble, it's the five of us against the world.' He grins. 'And you know what? It's going to be tongue in cheek all the way!'

69

BAND SCHEDULE

A typical few days for the new pop stars

Wednesday 15 November

14:00 Arrive at new house
Rules chat with Nigel
Sort out rooms/unpack

19:00 Interviews

21:00 Paul Adam arrives for chat

22:00 Norwegian producers arrive
for meeting

Thursday 16 November

AM Do weekly food shop for
the house

16:00 Meeting with Paul Adam
@ house

Friday 17 November

AM Nicki Chapman to come
and say hello @ house?

13:00 Travel to Holborn Studios,
London

14:00 Photoshoot with Ken McKay
and meet stylist

16:30 Finish and return to house

Saturday 18 November

Off to Sheffield to meet record
producer Elliot Kennedy

Sunday 19 November

Monday 20 November

Sheffield

Tuesday 21 November

Sheffield

Wednesday 22 November

Sheffield

Thursday 23 November

Sheffield

Friday 24 November

Return to London

Saturday 25 November

Sunday 26 November

Monday 27 November
? Meeting with record producer
Ray Hedges

WEEK 47

POPSTARS

	Monday						Sunday 26th
Edit 1 3	Off line						
Edit 2	Offline						
Edit 3	Digitising Poss promo	Poss promo					
Resolution	Offline 1+2 James	Offline 1+2 James	Offline 1+2 James				
Dub							
Voice Over							
Viewing Prep	Show 6 Dave Show 7 James	Show 6 Dave Show 7 James	Show 6 Dave Show 7 James	Show 6 Dave Show 7 James	Show 6 Dave Show 7 James		
Shoot	house 8 Danny	house 8 Danny	house 8 Danny	house 8 Danny	house 8 Danny		
Archiving							
Band	Sheffield louise & Danny	Isheffield louise & Danny	Sheffield louise & Danny	Sheffiled louise & Danny	Sheffield louise & anny	Return to London	In house
TX							

hear'say

On a dark, damp Tuesday in early February Danny, Myleene, Kym, Noel and Suzanne gather for their first all-day photo shoot. The studio in south-east London is teeming with people. The band's manager Chris Herbert is there, along with promotions and A&R people from their record company Polydor. There's stylist Juice and her assistant hairstylist Martin Gayle and his team, the make-up artist for the shoot and photographer Sandrine Dulermo and her team. And, to top it all, the Popstars production crew are all there to document the first time the newly styled Popstars band has ever been seen together.

The transformation is striking. Suzanne loves her new waist-length hair and glamorous look while Kym has a vivid red streak in her fringe. In the freezing studio, only Danny is not feeling the cold (in fact he's spent so much time next to the brazier full of flames that he's boiling!) and Noel's feet are killing him, as they've been squashed into a pair of trainers two sizes too small. Myleene, as ever, is taking it all in her stride.

It's really hard work and the band are constantly surrounded by people but they know that what will come out of the long day is the image that will introduce HEAR'SAY to the world.

Firstly, I would like to say a massive thank you to all my family + friends (you know who you are!) because of your love, trust + support, I am the individual I am today. I also want to thank all that have + have not supported me as both played a vital role in my determination. Lastly, I want to thank Noel, Suzanne, Kym + Mylene, you are all special individuals.

Be lucky, Danny.

I would like to thank the following people for helping me achieve my goal = Mum & Dad for being so so special, My big sister Tracy, big brothers David & Jon and all their families, My boyfriend Martin & his family, My best friend Tracy & family, Aunties & Uncles, and finally My two children David & Emily, you are my world!!! I love you all, thanks to all the above people for being you!!! xxx

Kym (Mummy)
xx - xxx

A Big big thank you to-Mum & Daddy-"the arrow finally hit something", My lil sister Chezzie-"God bless da mista, lil bro Don-"you are so wonderful"-Mahal kita X, Davey-My action hero-you are my eight X, Marlain-GC all da way!, the Goddess Symonie - Macaronie, Richard M-alias Batman, Oh Carolina, Claves., Mary Hammond "look no make up!", The Gorgeous Annie Skates, Paul Kirvage-for believing, Miss Wright & Mr. Hardy.
I love you all very very much.

Myleenie
X

Big thanks to my family + friends who have had faith and supported me throughout my career, You've been FAB! Thanks to my mum who deserve's an oscar for her efforts in making my dreams come true. Thanks to Andrew who has been around throughout the best + worst of times giving me the advice I've needed. finally to my new best friends + work colleagues, I couldn't have wished for a better bunch. Thanks everyone, love you all very much.

Suzanne X

I now know that thankyou is not a big enough word.!! Firstly, mum, my inspiration and support always. I'd be nothing without you and our angels, I LOVE YOU. My family, Cath, Mark, Luke & Joel be strong, big Cwtches×. My friends (you know who you are!) thanks for open ears & kind advice, I love you too! To everyone who doubted my ability and personality... who's laughing now ☺
And finally, Thanks to Danny, Mylene, Kym and Suzanne, my new family.... LET'S SHOW 'EM!!!!

Love to all
Noël×

Noel with cousins Joel (left) and Luke.

Photograph by Sheila Antoniazzi.

The Band would like to send out a special thank-you to the following people for thier hard work and support — Nigel Lythgoe - Nice mullet, Paul Adam — You're absolutely key!, Nikki Chapman - just 'BRILLIANT'. — we wont let you down — All the guys at LWT who produced such a top programme, all the producers we've been lucky enough to work with - what a total honour.
James Sulley - Guide us oh wise one, Chris Herbert & all the team at Safe - Thank God we found you!, Lucas - Rinky Dink - the 6th member of our band, Lou Cowmeadow - Drink plenty of water & Maria Malone — Turner prize here we come! what a team!

Finally a big 'hello' to all the people who auditioned for Popstars. It was an amazing experience where friends were made and exceptional talent was seen. Love n luck to you all.

Myleene X   Danny   Kym XX

Noël X   Suzanne X

80